Y0-EHU-088

The Associated Press

TWENTIETH-CENTURY Shipwrecks

A PICTORIAL HISTORY

TWENTIETH-CENTURY Shipwrecks
A PICTORIAL HISTORY

A NORBACK BOOK

BY DAN PERKES
WITH THE
**EDITORS OF THE
ASSOCIATED PRESS**

Contemporary Books, Inc.
Chicago

Library of Congress Cataloging in Publication Data

Perkes, Dan.
Twentieth-century shipwrecks.

1. Shipwrecks. I. Associated Press. II. Title.
III. Title: 20th century shipwrecks.
G525.P47 1983 363.1'23'0904 83-18939
ISBN 0-8092-5575-8

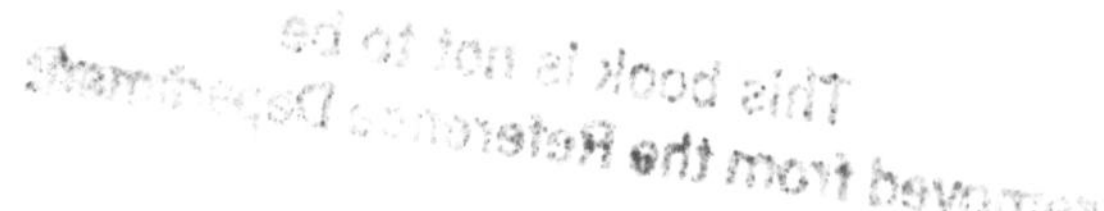

Published by Contemporary Books, Inc.
180 North Michigan Avenue, Chicago, Illinois 60601
Manufactured in the United States of America
Library of Congress Catalog Card Number:
International Standard Book Number: 0-8092-5575-8

Published simultaneously in Canada by Beaverbooks, Ltd.
195 Allstate Parkway, Valleywood Business Park
Markham, Ontario L3R 4T8 Canada

Contents

Foreword

The Poet Laureate John Masefield once wrote:

"I must go down to the seas again,
  to the lonely sea and the sky,
And all I ask is a tall ship
  and a star to steer her by . . ."

For more than 9,000 years—long before shepherds drove their flocks of sheep across the countryside or tilled the soil to make their daily bread—sailors have been steering their frail ships across stormy seas, at first with only the stars to guide them.

The seas and oceans were the links to the rest of the strange and unknown world of early civilization, so it became inevitable that man would cast his bread upon those waters to seek new adventure and riches.

The Phoenicians built an empire on sea trade; the Vikings took to longboats to plunder the coasts of Europe and implant their culture in England and in many areas of the European continent. Later, Italian, Portuguese, Dutch, and Spanish galleons would crisscross the seas and oceans of the world, charting new lands and bringing back to their mother countries the treasures of the Orient and the Americas. England, an island nation whose lifeblood was the ocean, would use her ships to build a global domain on which the sun never set until recent times.

But if these hearty sailors loved the sea, they feared her as well, for their gods—Poseidon to the early Greeks, Njord, Aegir, and Ran to Norwegian sailors—and all their prayers could not help those souls who went down to the sea in ships and never returned. The rotted wood carcasses and rusted iron and steel hulks of their ships litter the bottoms of the oceans and seas from Cape Horn to the Molucca Straits, from the Nantucket shoals to the cold Baltic.

Travel by sea has always been fraught with peril, danger, and awesome fear. In ancient times, man stood little chance against the elements—storms, fires, icebergs. Modern technology has given us the use of radar equipment, more accurate storm warnings, vast advances in ship construction, efficient ship-to-ship communication; yet there exists still that poignantly real possibility of disaster at sea.

This, then, is a book about twentieth-century shipwrecks—of particular interest because even these intricately designed, massive, and modern boats are subject to human error and the unpredictably violent elements. The true tales of recent disasters depicted on these pages occurred on lakes, rivers, and at sea, involving luxury liners, steamers, submarines, and pleasure cruisers. Words were able to describe the terrible events, but it took the eye of the camera to give new dimension to the horror.

The Editors

The Associated Press

TWENTIETH-CENTURY Shipwrecks

A PICTORIAL HISTORY

When God's great voice assembles
The fleet on Judgement Day,
The ghosts of ruined ships will rise
In sea and strait and bay.

The White Ships and The Red,
by Joyce Kilmer

THE FIRST HALF-CENTURY

The Devil's Handshake at Hell Gate

The *General Slocum* was considered an "unlucky" ship by those who knew her.

Commissioned in April of 1891 as an excursion steamer to handle the New York City trade, she was larger than most excursion boats—264 feet long, she had a 37-foot beam and side paddles measuring 31 feet in diameter.

But less than two months after going into service, the *Slocum*, named after a Civil War general, suffered her first mishap when a young woman was crowded off the deck and drowned. The next day, the steamer ran aground at Rockaway Inlet; then two days later she collided with another ship while docking on the Hudson River. A number of other accidents plagued the *Slocum* during the next several years.

Moreover, *Slocum*'s owners and captain had kept the boat in disrepair. Lifejackets and fire hoses were rotted with age; the lifeboats, seldom used, were frozen to chocks by coat after coat of old paint. Even the crew, most of them longshoremen with little shipboard experience, had never been adequately trained for emergencies.

More than 600 persons perished on June 28, 1904, when the ship *Norge* sank off Rockall Reef, Scotland.

The inventor of diving bells, in the 17th century, was one Edward Bendall of Massachusetts. He thus was the first underwater diver.

When the galleon *Mary Rose* sank (blown up by her own gunpowder) in Boston Harbor on July 27, 1640, Bendall took it upon himself to investigate. He described these newly constructed diving bells as "two great tubs, bigger than a butt, very tight, and open at one end upon which there hanged so many weights as would sink it to the ground."

Bendall rightly asked the General Court for a patent. Although no one in America had ever constructed such a device before, he was refused.

But neither these dangers nor the reputation of the ship were of concern to the nearly 1,500 passengers—mostly women and children—cruising down New York City's East River on June 15, 1904, for the annual outing sponsored by St. Mark's German Lutheran Church.

As Capt. W. H. Van Schaick headed his boat through Hell Gate, the narrowest passage along the East River, the skipper of a nearby barge noticed smoke trailing the *Slocum* and sounded four blasts of his whistle as a warning.

The fire, which apparently started in a midship storeroom, was reported to the captain, but no immediate action was taken. When the crewmen finally did move, their efforts were ineffectual. In fact, instead of sealing off the blaze, they opened portholes and doors which only served to fan the flames.

The *General Slocum* continued steaming ahead at full speed, even though rescue lay only one hundred yards away on the Bronx shore. Captain Van Schaick would later claim that he feared the fire would spread to wooden buildings ashore and hoped to ground the boat on North Brother Island a few miles down the river.

In their panic to escape the blaze, hundreds of passengers rushed to the rear of the boat, sweeping dozens of their fellow picnickers into the swirling river currents. By the time the *Slocum* was grounded on the rocks off North Brother Island, hundreds of other passengers were left dead in its wake.

In all, 1,021 lost their lives. One of the survivors was Captain Van Schaick, who would be tried for criminal negligence and sentenced to ten years in prison. He was later paroled and died at the age of 90 in a Utica, New York, Masonic Home.

But the memory of that tragedy still lingers. In Lutheran Cemetery in a quiet section of southern Queens lie 61 unidentified victims from the *General Slocum.* Nearby, headstones mark the graves of more than 900 others who perished on that bright spring day.

General Slocum

The burned-out hulk of the excursion steamer *General Slocum* was all that remained after she burned on New York's East River during an outing in June of 1904, with heavy loss of life. Her captain, W. H. Van Schaick, later was sent to prison for criminal negligence.

Bodies of some of the victims of the *General Slocum* excursion boat disaster on New York's East River are laid out on nearby ground shortly after the fire tragedy. The disaster claimed 1,021 lives, mostly women and children on a church outing. Sixty-one of the victims were never identified.

The Unsinkable

She was billed as the world's "safest" ship and unsinkable because of her new system of watertight doors.

She was the *Titanic,* luxurious pride of the White Star Line, embarked from Southampton, England, on April 10, 1912, for her maiden voyage across the North Atlantic to New York.

The liner boasted the new wireless radio, a theater, tennis and squash courts, Turkish baths, four restaurants plus the main dining room, a miniature golf course, and a dog kennel. What more could her blue-chip passenger list ask for?

More than 1,500 passengers would enjoy these posh accommodations on the *Titanic*'s debut crossing. In addition, more than 700 immigrants boarded her as steerage passengers.

Capt. E. T. Smith hoped to set a new crossing record for *Titanic* and kept his speed at twenty-two knots. He had received some warnings about icebergs in the shipping lanes, but the first five days at sea were sunny and the visibility was excellent.

On the night of April 14, *Titanic* had entered the

The sidewheel steamer, *Larchmont,* was literally twice the size of the coal schooner, *Harry Knowlton.* But when, on February 11, 1907, as the *Larchmont* proceeded south from Providence, Rhode Island, to New York City she was struck by the *Harry Knowlton,* she was nearly cut in two. As a result, 180 lives were lost.

The liner *Titanic,* pride of the White Star fleet. She was billed as the world's "safest" ship and unsinkable because of its new system of watertight doors. Among other things, on board were a theater, tennis courts, and even a dog kennel.

Grand Banks area off Newfoundland when a lookout spotted an iceberg. But the warning came too late and the giant liner sideswiped the iceberg. Only a slight bump was felt, but in that brief moment the floe had torn a fatal 300-foot gash below the ship's waterline.

The *Titanic*'s radio began sending distress signals, but the signals went unanswered. Inexplicably, a ship spotted on the horizon sailed away, ignoring both the radio calls as well as distress flares. That ship was later identified as the *Californian.* Its radio operator had turned off his radio receiver and had gone to sleep moments before the *Titanic* struck the iceberg.

Nearly an hour after the *Titanic* began taking on water, her first lifeboats were lowered. Because of the list, a number of boats could not be released from their davits. Others pulled away from the ship only half-filled with passengers.

Shortly after 2:00 A.M., the *Titanic*'s stern rose high above the cold waters, and in a burst of bubbles, sank beneath the waves, taking with her some 1,500 souls.

Among the prominent passengers who died were Benjamin Guggenheim, Col. John Jacob Astor (although his wife survived); Maj. Archibald W. Butt, President Taft's military aide; Frank D. Millet, the renowned American painter; William T. Stead, a leading British journalist; and Henry B. Harris, the noted Broadway producer. In addition to Mrs. Astor, those who were lucky enough to escape the sea included Robert Daniel, a highly successful, multimillionaire Philadelphia banker; Sir Cosmos Duff Gordon and his wife, Lady Duff Gordon; and the Countess of Rothes.

Later, an official inquiry would find the White Star Line negligent, with only enough lifeboats for little more than 1,100 people. The crew also was cited for lack of training and discipline. And the captain, who went down with his ship, was condemned for pushing the *Titanic* to excessive speeds despite the iceberg warnings.

Two years later, as a result of the disaster, the U.S. Coast Guard established the first iceberg patrols of the North Atlantic.

The ill-fated *Titanic* is shown departing Southampton, England, for the start of her maiden voyage across the North Atlantic to New York. Aboard were more than 1,500 passengers, including some from among the wealthiest families in America. Capt. E. T. Smith hoped to set a new crossing speed record.

Titanic

This is an artist's conception of the sinking of *Titanic,* which went down off Newfoundland April 15, 1912, after striking an iceberg. It was one of the sea's greatest disasters; 1,513 were lost of whom 103 were women and 53 were children. Capt. E. T. Smith went down with his ship.

Crowds gathered around the bulletin board of the *New York American* in New York City for the latest news of prominent people who were rescued from the sinking *Titanic.*

Great crowds also gathered outside of the White Star Line in New York to seek news of missing friends, relatives, and business associates who were on the *Titanic.* The inset shows Mrs. Benjamin Guggenheim, wife of the smelter millionaire, leaving the steamship office after seeking news of her husband.

Within Sight of Land

The *Lusitania* was Great Britain's "Queen of the Seas" and the pride of her merchant marine. She was a big, graceful ship—785-foot sister of the old *Mauretania*—and she held the blue ribbon for fast Atlantic crossings.

The *Lusitania* had sailed from New York on May 1, 1915, despite warnings from the German government that all passengers would be traveling at great risk since England and Germany were at war.

The noted playwright Charles Klein said before sailing that he was not concerned. He said he planned to spend his time aboard ship thinking of his new play, *Postash and Perlmutter in Society.*

And Elbert Hubbard, famous publisher of the magazine *Philistine,* joked that if the ship was torpedoed he would be able to do justice to the Kaiser in his publication.

So the great liner sailed for England, with 1,968 passengers and crew, to the cheers of hundreds at her dock, despite Germany's policy, announced just a few days before, of unrestricted submarine warfare.

The passengers had good reason to be secure.

The *Lusitania* was double-bottomed and she had 170 water-tight compartments which could be closed automatically in a few seconds.

On the afternoon of May 7, a bright, sunny day, *Lusitania* was in sight of the Irish coast, when a startling message broke the humdrum routine of the wireless station at Land's End, England.

"Come at once," the radio crackled in dots and dashes. "Big list. Position 10 miles south of Kinsale."

Lusitania's passengers had just finished their midday meal when a lookout spotted the first torpedo. Capt. William T. Turner watched the wake made by the deadly missile as it neared, but it was too late to do anything about it. The torpedo drilled into the forward section of the starboard side. Seconds later, another torpedo struck amidships near the boilers.

Within moments a tremendous explosion rocked the ship. As water poured into gaping holes, *Lusitania* staggered and listed and began settling by the head. In a few seconds, it was virtually impossible to stand on the decks.

Because of the list, it was also impossible to get all life boats into the water. In less than 20 minutes, the great ship had slipped beneath the sea's surface, drowning 1,198 persons, including 128 Americans.

The water was dotted with men and women clinging to floating wreckage. And there were also the dead. Captain Turner was the last to leave the ship. He walked calmly down a ladder as the ship went under. He clung to a floating chair for two hours until he was picked up by a rescue boat.

There were many incidents of quiet bravery in that quick rendezvous with death.

The American millionaire, Alfred Gwynne Vanderbilt, whose body never was recovered, took off his own life preserver and handed it to a hysterical woman. He was last heard to say to a fellow passenger, "Let's go below and see if there are any kiddies left."

Playwright Klein would never have to worry about his play; he perished, along with publisher Hubbard and Hubbard's wife.

The Spanish steamer *Principe de Asturias* struck a reef near Sebastian Point off the northern coast of Spain and sank, with more than 500 dead, on March 5, 1912. In that same year, on September 28, more than 1,000 passengers and crew went down with the Japanese steamer *Kichemaru* off the coast of Japan.

On May 29, 1914, the steamer *Empress of Ireland,* owned by the Canadian Pacific Lines, collided with a Norwegian collier in the St. Lawrence River, sending 1,024 passengers and crew to their doom.

At the headquarters of *The Associated Press* in New York and throughout the service, editors and reporters worked under an extra strain. All knew that Herbert S. Stone, son of AP General Manager Melville E. Stone, was a *Lusitania* passenger. He was among those who did not survive.

Except for the violation of Belgium's neutrality, no one act of the First World War did so much to alienate from Germany the sympathy of the neutral world.

The effect in the U.S. was tremendous. It could be read in the headlines of many leading newspapers:

"Slaughter Of The Neutrals."

"Premeditated And Dastardly."

"A Diabolical Outrage."

Theodore Roosevelt branded the sinking as "the greatest act of piracy in history."

In Germany, however, there was celebration. Grand Adm. Alfred Von Tirpitz received hundreds of telegrams of congratulations, and children decorated school houses and were given a half-day holiday.

Official Washington was stunned. President Woodrow Wilson cancelled engagements and walked alone, pondering the gravity of the situation. There were prayers in the churches asking for divine guidance for the President. There were clamors for stern action, and there were many demands for an immediate declaration of war. But pacifists and proponents of the doctrine of "peace at any price" continued to plead their case.

As time passed and Germany made no complete apology (it did cable sympathy for the loss of American lives, but at the same time maintained that the responsibility was Great Britain's), the desire to join the war in many sections of the country began to take tangible form and estrangement between America and Germany became pronounced.

Even today, many historians agree that the sinking of the *Lusitania* was an important and influential factor in bringing the United States into the "war to end all wars."

Lusitania

The *Lusitania* is seen sailing from New York on May 1, 1915.

NEW YORK, SATURDAY, MAY 8, 1915.—TWENTY-FOUR PAGES.

LUSITANIA SUNK BY A SUBMARINE, PROBABLY 1,260 DEAD; TWICE TORPEDOED OFF IRISH COAST; SINKS IN 15 MINUTES; CAPT. TURNER SAVED, FROHMAN AND VANDERBILT MISSIN[G]; WASHINGTON BELIEVES THAT A GRAVE CRISIS IS AT HA[ND]

[SH]OCKS THE PRESIDENT

[W]ashington Deeply Stirred by the Loss of American Lives.

[B]ULLETINS AT WHITE HOUSE

[W]ilson Reads Them Closely, but is Silent on the Nation's Course.

[HI]NTS OF CONGRESS CALL

[L]oss of Lusitania Recalls Firm Tone of Our First Warning to Germany.

CAPITAL FULL OF RUMORS

The Lost Cunard Steamship Lusitania

X Where the First Torpedo Struck. XX Where the Second Torpedo Struck.

Canard Office Here Besieged for News; Fate of 1,918 on Lusitania Long in Doubt

Nothing Heard from the Well-Known Passengers on Board—Story of Disaster Long Unconfirmed While Anxious Crowds Seek Details.

List of Saved Includes Capt. Turner; Vanderbilt and Frohman Reported Lost

Saw the Submarine 100 Yards Off and Watched Torpedo as It Struck Ship

Ernest Cowper, a Toronto Newspaper Man, Describes Attack, Seen from Ship's Rail—Poison Gas Used in Torpedoes, Say Other Passengers.

SOME DEAD TA[KEN]

Several Hund[red] ... ors at Que[enstown] and Kin[sale]

STEWARD TELLS ...

SHIP LISTS OV[ER]

ATTACKED IN ...

A reproduction of the front page of *The New York Times,* May 8, 1915. The "X" marks indicate where the first, then second, torpedo struck.

A broadside view of the ship, Great Britain's "Queen of the Seas."

Pride of the Great Lakes

Although she was reputed to be a "cranky" ship, the passenger steamer *Eastland* had seen twelve good years of service on the Great Lakes and could hit thirty knots or so per hour, making her one of the fastest ships in the Lakes area.

But her steel hull was light, her superstructure heavy and her shape narrow, giving her a reputation for instability. On some occasions, in fact, crewmen had to herd frightened passengers from one side of the vessel to the other to correct a dangerous list.

Nevertheless, the 265-foot *Eastland* looked mighty impressive in her Chicago River berth near the Clark Street Bridge on that Saturday morning, July 24, 1915.

A happy crowd of about 7,000 people—employees of the Western Electric Company and their families—waited to board the *Eastland* and four other ships for the company's annual outing to Michigan City and the Indiana dune country.

An estimated 2,500 picnickers had crowded on board, and Capt. Harry Pedersen, the *Eastland*'s master, ordered the engineer to trim ship by partially

One of the oddest unsolved shipwrecks is that of the tug, *Wm. Maloney*. On November 15, 1924, she began to steam from Newton Creek in Brooklyn to Newport, Rhode Island, apparently in search of work.

It is known that a major storm took place at sea on November 16, and the tug and her crew of 12 disappeared without a trace.

Until a relative inquired about one of the crew members the following January, no search was ever begun. In February the Coast Guard decided to address the New York office of Customs Service, only to discover that no one was interested. The case was dropped without ever having had even a preliminary investigation.

By 1927, the fate of the *Wm. Maloney* had been entirely forgotten and dismissed. There was never any reported wreckage, and no bodies were ever discovered to have washed up on any beach.

On November 12, 1928, the British ship *Vestris,* steaming from New York to Buenos Aires, was fighting heavy seas off the Virginia capes. Her cargo of heavy equipment suddenly shifted and the ship listed badly to starboard. The *Vestris'* skipper, Capt. William Carey, who later would be blamed for the disaster, mistakenly ordered pumping of the wrong ballast tank, thereby dooming the ship. Of the 197 crew and 128 passengers, 110 people—including the captain—perished.

filling the port ballast tanks. The bow line was freed, and the ship drifted sideways into the river, its stern line still fastened to the dock.

Suddenly, the *Eastland* listed sharply to port, but soon righted herself. Then the ship again heeled to port and hundreds of passengers started sliding across the sloping deck, canted at almost a forty-five degree angle. Crewmen tried to drive the panicked passengers back to starboard, but the incline already was too steep for them. Below deck, hundreds of other passengers started clawing one another in an effort to make it up the companionway.

Then the worst happened. The weight of the *Eastland*'s list snapped the stern line and the ship rolled over.

The anguished cries of the crowd ashore mixed with the screams of the *Eastland*'s passengers as hundreds were thrown into the murky waters of the Chicago River.

Children bobbed like corks on the water, then disappeared; some passengers swam to shore. Those who could not swim screamed in terror before disappearing in the turgid waters.

Of the estimated 2,500 happy picnickers who had climbed onto *Eastland*'s gangway that day, 812 found that death took an outing with them. The victims included twenty-two entire families.

In the aftermath of the disaster, the finger of blame was pointed at many, including the *Eastland*'s owners, her captain, her crew as well as the original shipbuilders.

But the bitterest pill the survivors had to swallow came twenty years later when the courts held *Eastland*'s owners blameless and declared that the *Eastland* was seaworthy. Instead, blame was laid on the ship's engineer, who, the courts said, made a mistake by over-filling the ballast tanks.

Later, the overturned vessel was raised, repaired, and sold to the federal government. Rechristened as the U.S.S. *Wilmette,* she served as a naval training ship until she was towed up the Chicago River and scrapped in 1946.

Eastland

Survivors clamber over the hull of the passenger steamer *Eastland,* which capsized in the Chicago River. An estimated 2,500 picnickers had crowded onto the ship's decks when the tragedy occurred. Death claimed 812 lives.

The Chicago River tug *Kenosha* helped in the rescue of survivors from the steamer *Eastland* after she had capsized at her mooring. Many of the victims were trapped below decks when the ship turned turtle.

Dozens of rescue boats surround *Eastland,* while hundreds of searchers comb her decks for survivors. The accident claimed 812 lives, but rescue operations continued for days after the last body was found. Note the thousands of onlookers lining both sides of the Chicago River.

(Top) Rescuers haul out the body of a woman, one of many victims found in the lower decks of the Great Lakes steamer *Eastland,* which overturned at her berth on the Chicago River on July 24, 1915. The bottom photo shows searchers continuing to remove additional bodies from the hull.

These photos show salvage operations on the *Eastland*. The overturned vessel eventually was raised, repaired, and later sold to the federal government to be used as a Naval training ship during World War II. In 1946, she was towed back up the Chicago River and scrapped.

Jinx Ship

The fast and luxurious Ward Line passenger ship *Morro Castle* was known as a jinx ship among sailors. Once she nearly grounded off Cape Hatteras. Another time she was caught in a crossfire between rebel and government forces in Havana Harbor. She also suffered a series of mysterious fires in the hold area.

Her luck hadn't changed as she bucked a stiff nor'easter off the New Jersey coast on the night of September 7, 1934, as she neared completion of another Havana to New York pleasure cruise.

Her captain, Robert Wilmott, had suffered a fatal heart attack that night and command fell on the nervous first mate, William Warms. Last-night festivities had been cancelled because of the death, and most passengers were in bed by 2:30 A.M.

It was about that time that someone noticed a wisp of smoke curling from out of a locker in the writing room. Within a short time, *Morro Castle* was engulfed in flames. Of the 548 passengers and crewmen, 134 perished in the flames or by drowning.

The wreck of the *Morro Castle* was not the worst

In 1935, the wreck of the U.S. gundalow *Philadelphia* was raised intact from the bottom of Lake Champlain. This in itself is not unusual. What is unique is that the *Philadelphia* had been under water for more than 150 years.

The survival of a ship as wreck is principally dependent upon the nature of the water that surrounds her. Salt in the sea is a tremendous destroyer; consequently, ships that have gone down in fresh water are much better preserved. Another factor in preservation is the sea or water life itself: millions of microorganisms slowly eat away at the organic material of the ship.

marine tragedy in terms of lost lives' but in terms of lives wasted due to events that could have been prevented, this sad case ranks with the worst. Even today, nearly a half century later, the *Morro Castle* disaster leaves a legacy as one of the strangest, saddest, and most shameful in seafaring history. It left a record of incredible ineptitude on the part of the officers and crew, of tragic hysteria, of occasional heroism, yes, but mostly of prevailing cowardice.

The tragedy was one of confusion, negligence, and stupidity. Only perfunctory fire drills had been held during the voyage so as not to alarm the passengers, and discipline among the crewmen generally was poor. In fact, it was quite evident that many of *Morro Castle*'s crew knew little or nothing about their emergency duties. Fire doors, which might have contained the blaze, remained wide open, sucking in fire-fanning drafts. Even essential fire-fighting equipment was either missing or inoperable.

Passengers and many crewmen were not aroused until the ship was already doomed. Even longer was the delay in sending out an SOS. Second Radio Operator George Alagna would testify later that time after time he made the 50-foot trip from the radio shack to the bridge to get instructions from Warms to tap out a distress signal. And each time, Alagna said, he was ignored by the stunned first mate.

In the first six, half-empty lifeboats that were launched, only six were passengers; the 92 others aboard were crewmen.

The *Morro Castle,* abandoned by all except Acting Captain Warms and a small group of sailors who huddled on the bow of the stricken ship, was taken under tow by a smaller Coast Guard vessel. But the tow broke and the still-smoking gutted skeleton of the ship was washed up on the beach at Asbury Park, New Jersey. Acting Capt. William Warms survived the disaster. Subsequently he, along with Acting Second Officer Ivan Freeman, Chief Radio Operator George W. Rogers, and Acting First Officer George Hackney, were brought before a grand jury inquiry conducted by the Federal Bureau of Navigation. Warms was convicted of negligence but the decision was later reversed by the Federal Circuit Court of Appeals.

"Jinx" ship *Morro Castle* burns fiercely off the New Jersey coast after a fire of undetermined origin raged out of control. Of the 548 passengers and crewmen, 134 perished. The disaster was called one of the most shameful in maritime history.

One of the strangest episodes of the *Morro Castle* affair centered on Chief Radio Operator George W. Rogers, who first was hailed as a hero since he stayed at his post to send the distress signal, despite the conflagration around him. A chain of circumstances later indicated that Rogers may have been responsible for the tragedy in the first place.

It was found that Rogers had a history of crime dating back to the age of twelve. His record included arrests for sodomy, theft, and suspicion of arson. After the disaster, he joined the Bayonne, New Jersey, police department as a radio repairman, and in 1938 he was convicted of trying to blow up his immediate superior with a homemade bomb.

In 1953, he was sentenced to life in prison for the bludgeon slaying of an elderly printer and his daughter.

When he died in prison in 1958, Rogers was mourned by obituary writers as the hero of the *Morro Castle* who had gone bad.

Morro Castle

A lifeboat with survivors of the *Morro Castle* is shown as it approached a nearby rescue ship. In the first six lifeboats that were launched were only six passengers; 92 others were members of the crew.

The Coast Guard Cutter *Tampa* stands by the stricken vessel, ready to tow it into port. The acting captain and several crewmen of the *Morro Castle* remained on board.

A dying passenger from *Morro Castle* is carried ashore by lifeguards at Sea Girt, New Jersey. He died soon after drifting ashore from the burning ship. This victim had jumped overboard wearing only underwear and a life belt.

The fire-ravaged hulk of the *Morro Castle,* still smoking, washed ashore at Asbury Park, New Jersey. The ship was raked by flames virtually from stem to stern.

The still-smouldering remains of the *Morro Castle* tosses in the surf at Asbury Park more than 24 hours after burning at sea.

Crowds of the curious flocked to the Asbury Park beach as the Ward liner *Morro Castle* continued to smoulder. Fire hoses, visibly sagging in the water, were put aboard after two violent explosions were touched off by rupturing oil tanks. The building at left was the Asbury Park Convention Hall.

Twisted steel and charred paint offered mute testimony to the intensity of the fire that ravaged the *Morro Castle.* Essential fire-fighting equipment aboard ship either was missing or inoperable.

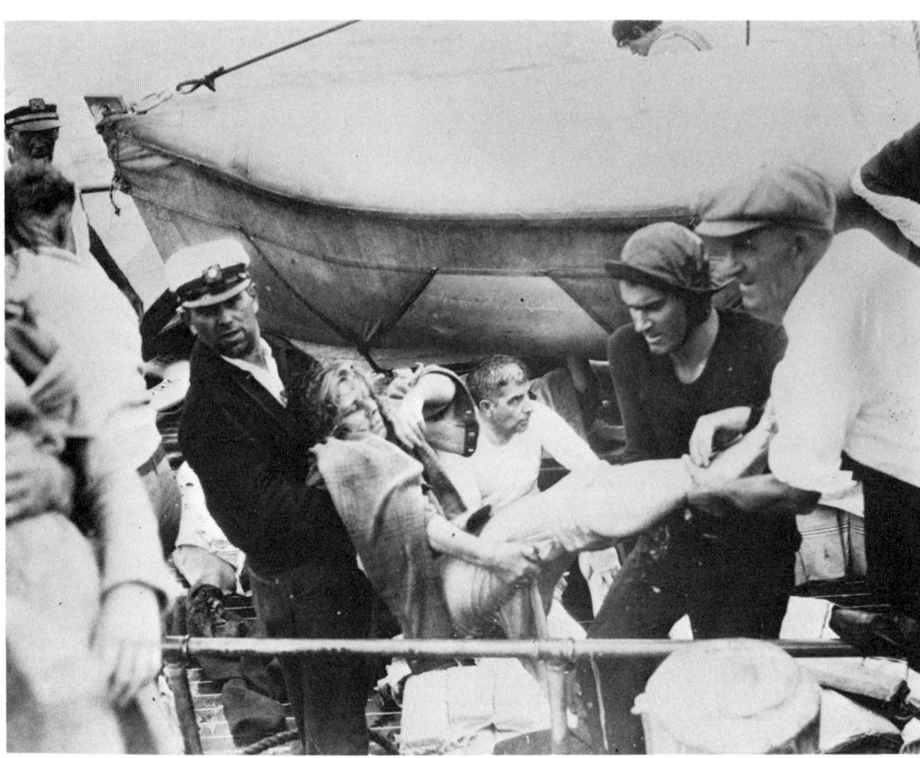

A woman survivor is taken off a small fishing boat at Manasquam, New Jersey, during the early morning hours of September 8. She is weak from exposure and submersion.

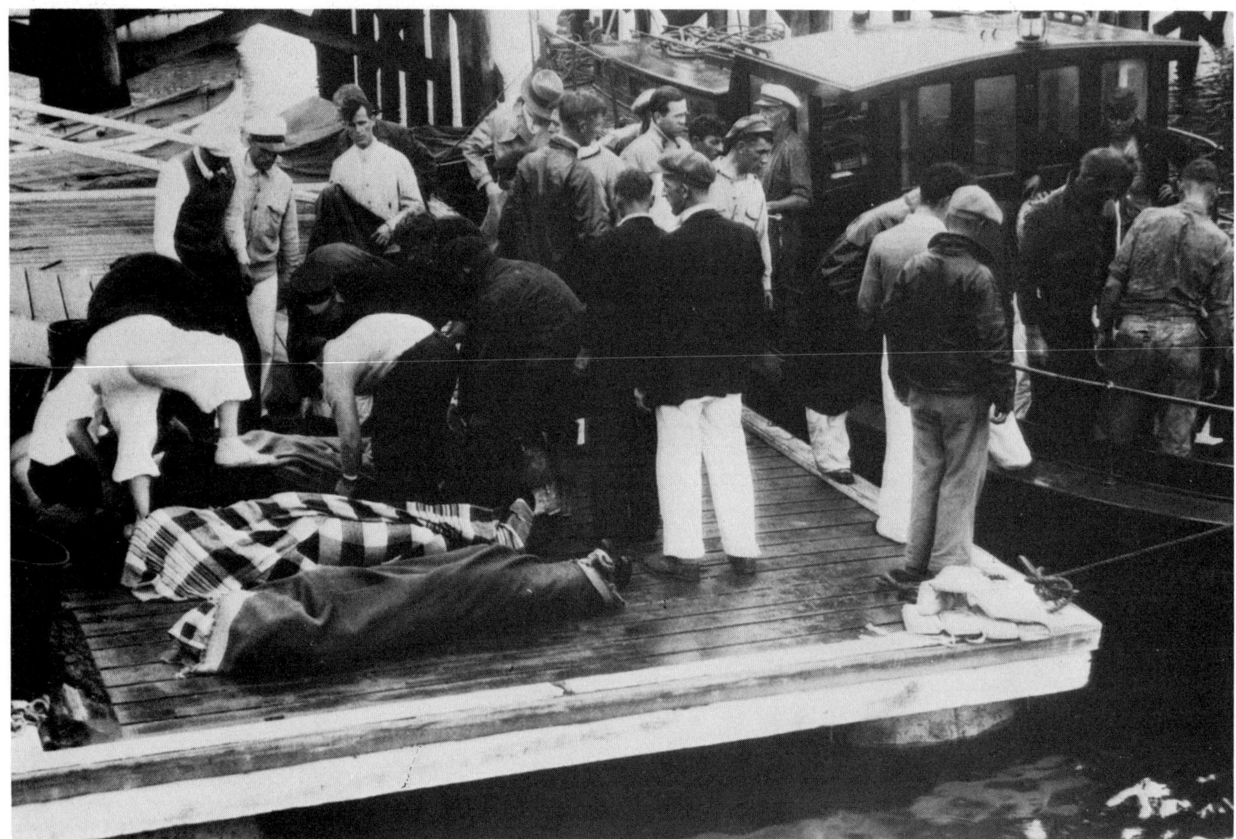

Bodies of several victims who died trying to escape the burning ship lay shrouded in blankets on an Asbury Park pier.

Four officers of the *Morro Castle* are shown during a grand jury inquiry conducted by the Federal Bureau of Investigation. From left: Acting Second Officer Ivan Freeman, Chief Radio Operator George W. Rogers, Acting Captain William Warms, and Acting First Officer George Hackney.

Nearly a year after the disaster, a salvage company at Baltimore, Maryland, started dismantling the *Morro Castle* piece by piece.

A Cruel Choice

Squalus, newest addition to the U.S. naval underwater fleet, sailed out of Portsmouth, New Hampshire, at 6:30 A.M. on May 23, 1939, for a series of shallow "crash dive" tests fifteen miles off the coast.

Squalus had begun her first dive at about 10:30 A.M. and was at fifty feet when the engine room began flooding, the result of a main air induction valve that had failed to close.

Lt. Oliver F. Naquin, the boat's skipper, ordered all bulkhead hatches sealed, and the cruelest duty of all fell to Electrician's Mate Lloyd Maness. He was nearest the hatch that separated the flooding aft section of *Squalus* from the forward section of the submarine.

Maness waited until the last possible moment, permitting passage of a few crewmen. Then, as seawater poured through the hatchway—and with not another second to spare—he slammed shut the hatch and sealed the fate of 26 others left behind.

As he did so, Maness recalled, "I thought of Sherman Shirley, my chum. I was to be best man at his wedding the next Sunday."

During World War II, the world's largest ship, the *Queen Mary,* had been converted to a troop carrier. On October 2, 1942, she was steaming at top speed on a zigzag course as part of a convoy off the coast of Ireland. On board were 10,000 American troops. Under sunny skies, with no enemy forces nearby, the *Queen Mary* suddenly struck the slower-moving British cruiser *Curacao* and cut her in half. No one was injured on the *Queen Mary,* but 338 crewmen of the cruiser died. Later, a court of inquiry would hold the captain of the *Curacao* to blame.

The U.S. Navy had seen its share of disasters, but none quite the size and scope of the one that struck Adm. William F. (Bull) Halsey's Third Fleet in the western Pacific on December 17–18, 1944. In this case, the Japanese were not the foe. After a decisive victory over the Japanese at the Battle of Leyte Gulf, Halsey took his ships to a refueling rendezvous 500 miles east of Luzon and ran right into a typhoon. Smaller ships fared the worst in the 125 mile-an-hour winds, with at least three destroyers capsizing. The storm did more damage to the U.S. Navy than any single battle of the war. Bull Halsey survived the typhoon, and inasmuch as he was hailed as a war hero, there were few who would publicly hold him responsible for the Luzon disaster.

The vestiges of World War II continued to create havoc long after the final shots had been fired. On January 10, 1947, for example, the Greek steamer *Himara* struck an old mine still afloat in the Saronic Gulf south of Athens and sank with a loss of 392 people.

The *Squalus* lay in 240 feet of water on the ocean bottom, and rescue operations were underway from the Portsmouth Naval Shipyard within minutes after she failed to report by radio. The salvage ship *Falcon,* carrying a 10-ton diving bell, left New London, Connecticut, and sped through the day and night to anchor over *Squalus* the following day.

It was to be many hours before a waiting nation would learn that thirty-three men were still alive in two forward compartments of the 310-foot submarine. And for two tension-filled days, the world's attention focused on a little spot in the Atlantic until those thirty-three survivors were brought to the surface by the rescue bell.

But the saga of *Squalus* wasn't over; next came the epic salvage of the boat. Until then, it was the deepest waters in which Navy divers had ever operated.

It took salvagers all summer, but finally on September 15 they raised the *Squalus* and towed it back to Portsmouth where the bodies of the trapped crewmen were removed.

The *Squalus,* refitted and re-christened as *Sailfish,* would go on to distinguished service in the Pacific during World War II, sinking more than 45,000 tons of Japanese shipping. Maness, the unfortunate Electrician's Mate who had to slam the hatch shut on his trapped crewmates of the *Squalus,* would serve a short time on *Sailfish.* He later transferred to another warship and was killed in action.

Naquin left submarine duty and was serving as chief engineer aboard the battleship *California* when she was bombed and torpedoed at Pearl Harbor, December 7, 1941. He would retire from the Navy in 1955 as a Rear Admiral.

Squalus

Navy officers and men rig pontoons and buoys in an attempt to raise the sunken submarine *Squalus* off Portsmouth, New Hampshire. *Squalus* was in 240 feet of water and a diving bell was able to rescue 33 of her crew.

The first salvage effort was unsuccessful. The bow of the *Squalus* shot out of the water, then broke its moorings and sank again, leaving tangled hose lines and damaged pontoons.

When the pontoons surged upward on the second attempt, the salvage crew knew that *Squalus* had pulled loose from the mud below. The sub then was towed to more shallow water.

Squalus slowly rises to her normal surface position as water is pumped from her hull in Portsmouth Navy Yard. As soon as the water was cleared, the bodies of 26 crewmen would be removed. The submarine, later refitted and rechristened as *Sailfish,* would see distinguished action against the Japanese in World War II.

A Last Pleasure Cruise

The Great Lakes region has seen its share of maritime disasters over the years, but few quite so tragic as that which involved the S.S. *Noronic.*

She was the largest of the pleasure ships then traveling the Great Lakes waters, and in the early morning hours of September 17, 1949, she sat comfortably moored at Queen's Quay in Toronto Harbor.

She was a magnificent sight. Her well-lit hull stretched 362 feet from bow to stern and her five decks towered majestically above the dockyard area.

Carrying 524 passengers and 171 crewmen, *Noronic* had begun her final voyage of the season in Detroit, had crossed Lake Erie to Cleveland, and then had spanned Lake Ontario for a one-night stop in Toronto.

By 1:30 A.M., most passengers were back aboard ship. Most were asleep below, others were attending one of several festive parties in progress, and still others were just strolling the decks.

Within fifteen minutes, however, a fire believed to have started in a linen closet, would sweep the

Noronic from stem to stern, reducing the ship to a gutted hulk.

Hundreds of passengers were able to escape in a frantic, screaming, pushing mob by jumping to the pier, into the water, or clambering over the rails to smaller boats alongside.

But 120 unfortunate others—including several entire families—would find only death as they sought to escape the heat, smoke, and flames. Firemen who got aboard the heat-twisted ship five hours after the fire began told of finding groups of charred bodies with their arms about each other.

A special government court of inquiry was set up to investigate the fire which destroyed the $5 million ship and took so many lives.

Some passengers blamed the ship's officers for lack of leadership in the crisis. In turn, crew members blamed the passengers for yielding to hysteria and panic in their attempt to flee the ship.

Although the government report condemned the ship's owners for failure to take proper precautions against fire, the Ontario Attorney General's office issued a statement claiming that evidence showed there was no foundation for any charges of criminal negligence against either the *Noronic*'s owners or her skipper.

In subsequent years, however, damage claims totaling nearly $3 million would be awarded by the courts to the survivors or to the families of victims.

Noronic

Noronic, largest of the Great Lakes cruise ships, is shown burning in Toronto harbor in the early morning hours of September 17, 1949.

Toronto firemen, atop ladders at left, and on ground, fight a losing battle as flames light up the night sky.

A woman passenger is lowered to safety by ropes from the bow of the *Noronic* during the height of the fire while another passenger awaits her turn.

Firemen continued to pour water into *Noronic*'s smouldering hull, but all that was left of this majestic ship was a gutted wreckage.

Burned and charred remains of the *Noronic* were all that remained, as firemen poked through the wreckage looking for victims.

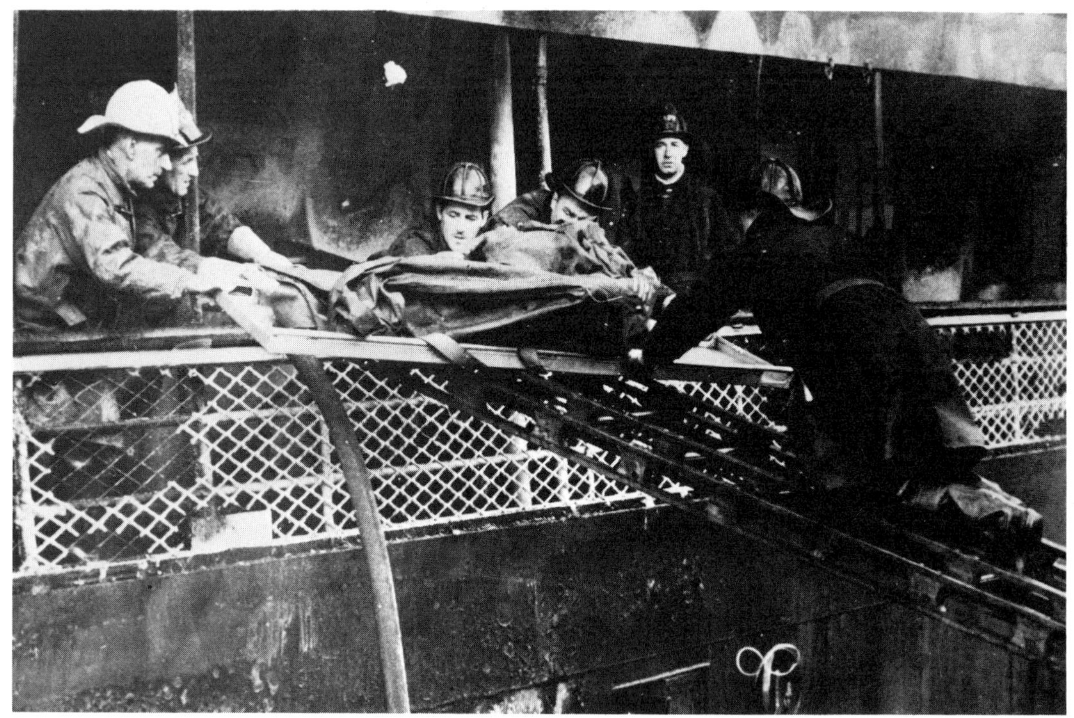

Firemen begin the grim task of removing bodies from the ship.

In many cases, bodies of fire victims were transported in police vans to the morgue. The burned-out ship is in the rear.

One of the last victims to be removed from the area was this man, whose body was recovered from the mud at the bottom of Toronto Bay three days later.

The Horticulture Building in downtown Toronto was set up as a makeshift morgue. Here investigators are shown inspecting clothing of the victims.

THE FIFTIES

No Escape

It was a simple training cruise for the British submarine *Affray*.

The 281-foot underwater boat was en route along the English Channel from Portsmouth to Falmouth, 180 miles to the southwest, and had been ordered to travel underwater all the way except between 8:00 A.M. and 9:00 A.M. each day, when she was to send a radio message. The trip began at 8:15 the morning of April 16, 1951, and was to have ended the following Thursday.

One of sixteen Royal Navy submarines of the "A" class, the 1,200-ton *Affray* was built in 1946 and spent two years of service in the Pacific. Returning home in 1948, she ran into a whale off Portugal and sliced it in two. The *Affray* suffered no damage.

For her last training exercise, she carried her regular crew of 51 officers and men. Also on board were 20 officers of the Royal Submarine School and four Marines. At least one of the men aboard, Sub. Lt. A. A. Frew, was a survivor of the submarine *Truculent,* which had sunk off the mouth of the Thames

River the previous year after a collision with a Swedish tanker. Sixty-four lives were lost on *Truculent.*

The *Affray* apparently suffered a fatal accident on the initial dive of its cruise off the Isle of Wight in the channel.

When the submarine hadn't reported in at its designated time, a massive sea and air search was launched.

American, French and Belgian naval vessels joined the British rescue fleet in crisscrossing the channel in an attempt to find the stricken sub. Nearly thirty hours after *Affray* was first reported missing, another British submarine, the *Sea Devil,* reported first word from the *Affray.* But the *Sea Devil* said the supersonic telegraph messages were too faint to be understood.

It was determined that *Affray* lay on the bottom of the channel in about 198 feet of water. Rescue

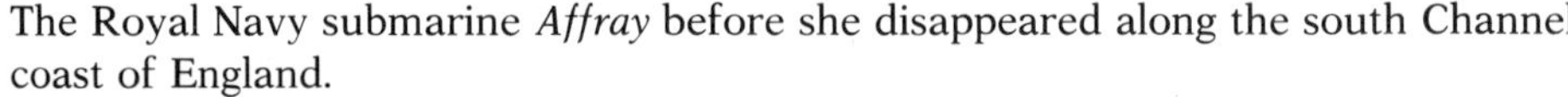

The Royal Navy submarine *Affray* before she disappeared along the south Channel coast of England.

ships hovered over the spot, but as the morning wore on there were no signs of any survivors making an attempt to use the sub's escape hatch.

An expert at the Admiralty said the *Affray* possibly could remain submerged without harm to her crew for forty hours unless she were badly damaged. Apparently she was, because the last faint signals were heard on the morning of the third day after her disappearance.

That evening, hope ran out for the seventy-five men entombed in the *Affray*. Even the most optimistic doubted that *Affray* had enough air left to keep anyone alive thirty fathoms down.

Admiralty officials speculated that the submarine's vital compartments had flooded during the dive, and that she lay on the seabed in a position which made the escape hatches not only unusable but inaccessible to any potential rescue divers.

Affray

Three nations joined in the search for the *Affray.* The British submarine *Amphion,* shown here, was one of the search vessels.

Lookouts aboard another vessel, the *Capable,* scrutinize everything afloat in their hunt for signs of the *Affray.*

RAF aircraft keep a close watch on the seas already alive with submarines, destroyers, rescue and detector crafts, all in search of the lost submarine.

June 1951 marked the date that the *Affray* was first identified by this underwater television camera inside its container.

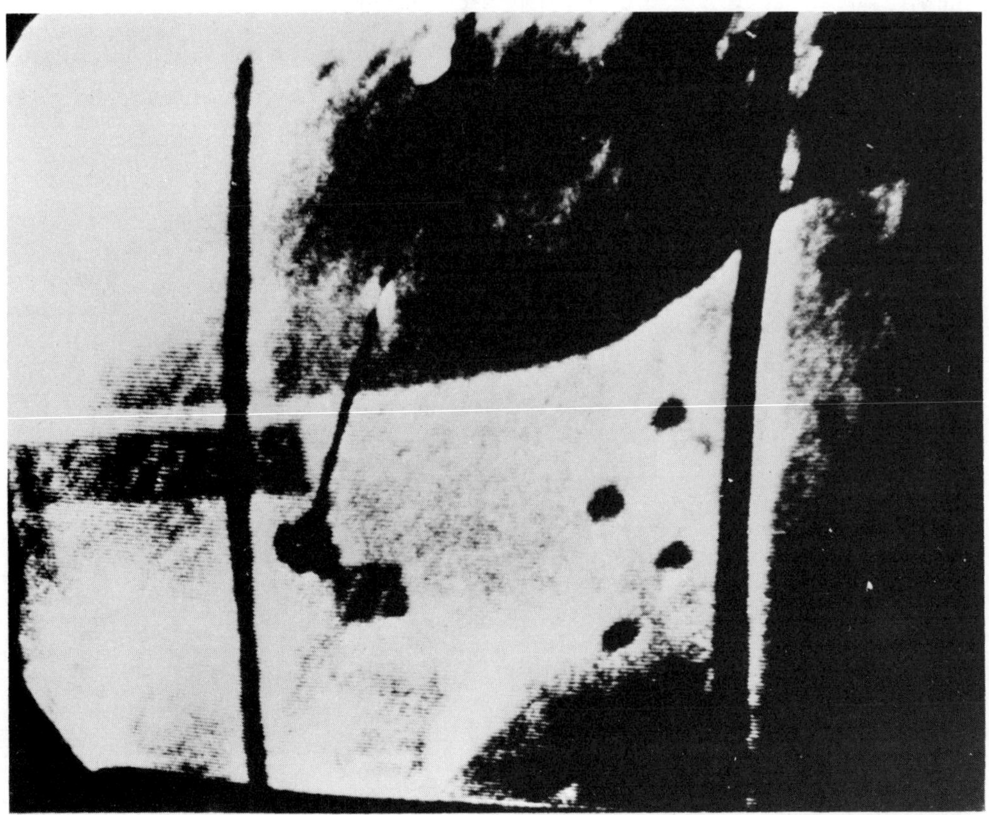

One view of the *Affray* through the television eye. The black oblong at left is the submarine's nameplate on which is imprinted the word *Affray*.

Death of a Hero

Both were heroes of World War II.

The U.S.S. *Hobson,* built as a destroyer and later converted to a fast minesweeper, started her fighting days early in the war. She helped with the landings at Casablanca in North Africa, took part in the strike at Bodo, Norway, and sank the German submarine U-575.

She was in on the Normandy landings in France and later got a unit citation for her work in the Atlantic Submarine Patrol. With her work in the Atlantic finished, the *Hobson* steamed into the Pacific and took part in the Okinawa campaign. During that action, she suffered severe wounds while downing several Japanese aircraft.

The carrier *Wasp,* namesake of the original *Wasp* sunk early in the Pacific war, also had a spectacular career during the World War II fighting, piling up blows against the enemy at Wake Island, Saipan, Tinian, Guam, and the Philippines, and in aerial attacks against the Japanese mainland. She also suffered damage during the war but was able to return to battle.

The typhoon has been one of the more destructive forces with which the peoples of Asia have lived for a millennium. One of the most destructive occurred on September 26, 1954, when it swept across Hakodate Bay in Japan. Spawning winds of more than 110 miles an hour, the storm sank over 1,000 small boats and killed 1,600. The greatest loss of life occurred when the harbor ferry *Toya Maru* sank and took 1,172 passengers to their death.

The 27,000-ton carrier *Wasp* under which the minesweeper *Hobson* sank on April 26, 1952.

18

On the night of April 26, 1952, both ships were part of a naval force streaming across the mid-Atlantic en route to the Mediterranean for peacetime duties. The fleet was just completing nighttime maneuvers and the *Wasp* was turning into the wind for aircraft landings. Suddenly, tragedy struck without warning on a rolling sea under faint stars and a black sky.

The *Hobson* found itself under the clifflike bows of the 27,000-ton carrier. The larger ship plowed into the starboard side of the minesweeper, cutting it literally in two. Within minutes, the *Hobson* sank.

Most of the *Hobson*'s men were trapped below decks, many in their bunks. Many were men who had never been to sea before.

The *Wasp* immediately launched eight small boats for rescue operations. Life jackets, rafts, floats, and nets were thrown over the side to help survivors struggling in the water. But 176 members of the *Hobson*'s crew, including her skipper, perished. Sixty-one others, including some severely injured, were saved in what was called the Navy's worst accident since World War II.

By dawn the next day, 14-knot winds were whipping across the littered water, but the search continued. As the day proceeded, winds picked up to gale force and word was passed that hope had been abandoned for any more survivors. The search was discontinued, and red-eyed and exhausted Navy men staggered to their bunks.

The *Wasp,* with all her aircraft aboard, reset her course for the Brooklyn Navy Yard for repairs of a 75-foot gash along her forward bow.

(Opposite page) An oil-covered James F. McIntyre, a survivor of the *Hobson,* is plucked from the sea following the disastrous collision.

Hobson

A lifeboat with three survivors of the *Hobson* is hoisted aboard the *Wasp*.

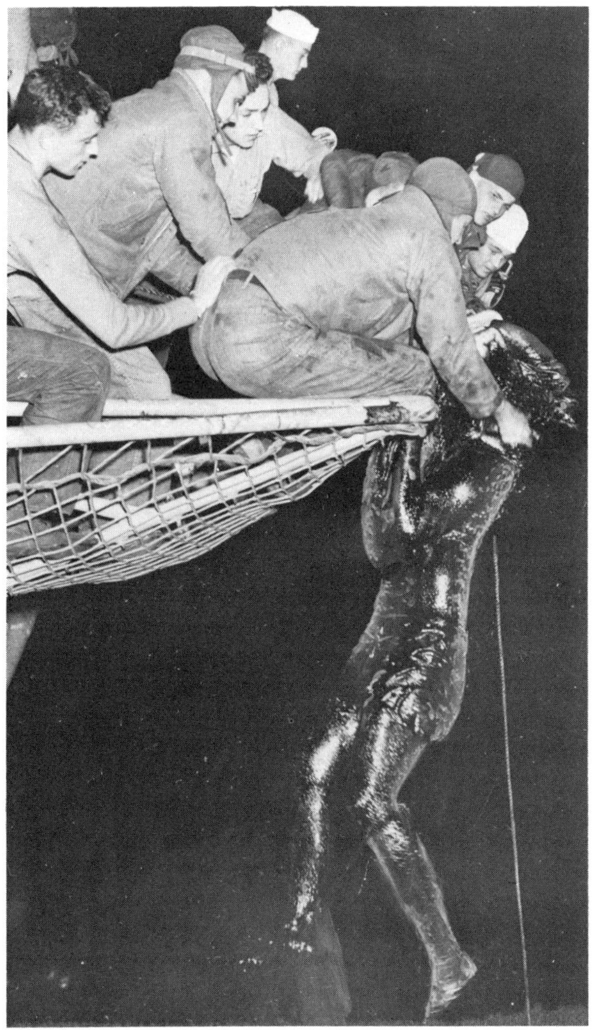

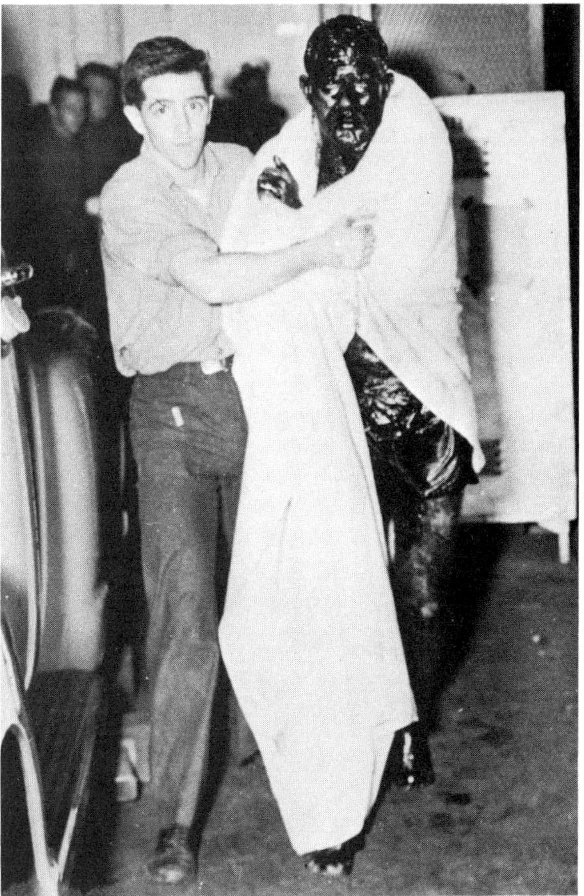

Russell L. Archer, another *Hobson* survivor, is assisted to the sick bay of the *Wasp*.

After having been saved from the *Hobson,* Cecil R. Myers (left) walks on deck the *Wasp.*

A close-up of the huge, knifelike, ripped bow of the *Wasp.*

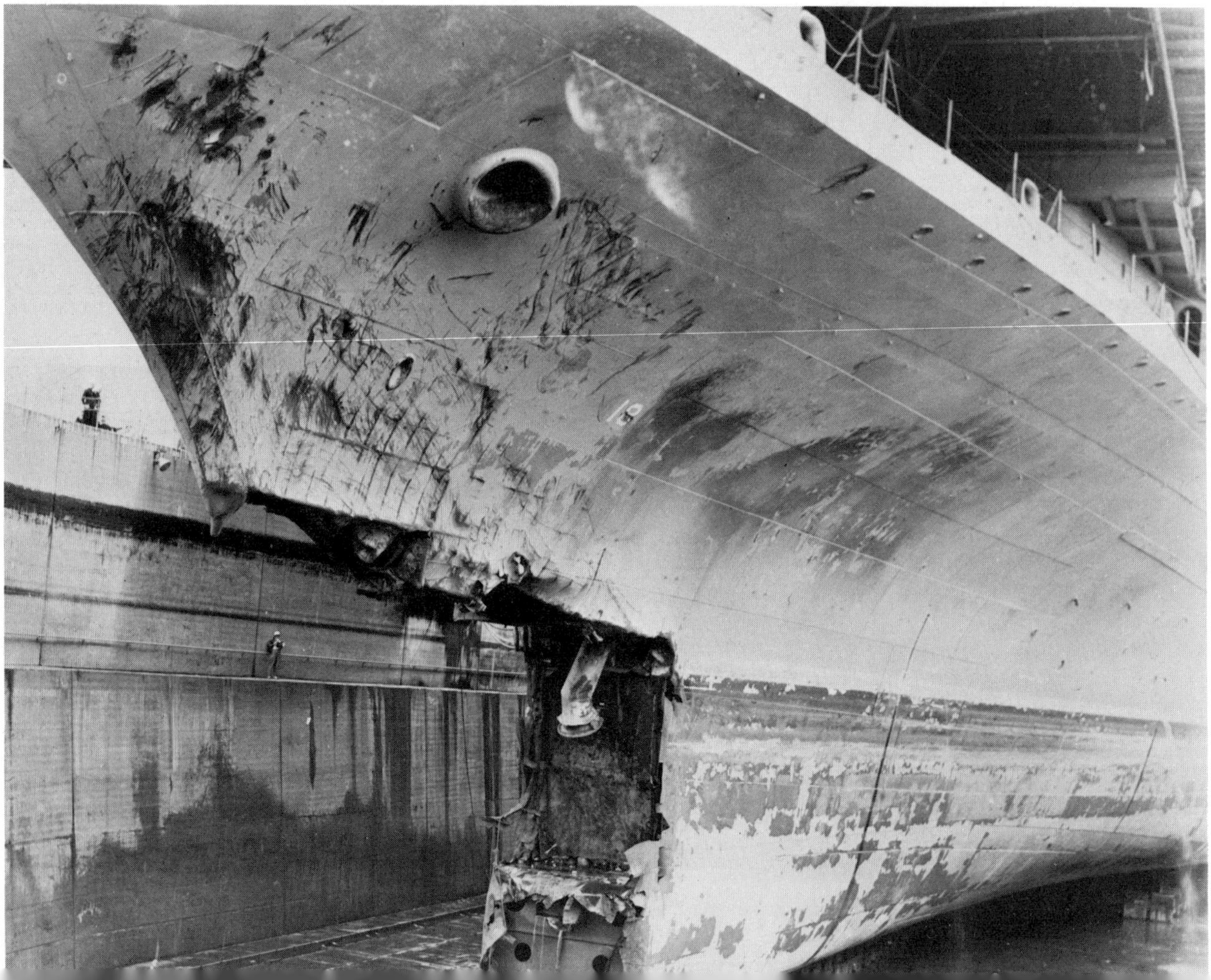

Divers prepare to go underwater to inspect the broken bow.

The sixty-one survivors of the ill-fated *Hobson* as they arrive in New York on May 6, 1952.

Andrea Doria

This artist's dramatic rendition is of two ships that failed to pass in the night—the $29 million liner *Andrea Doria* and the Swedish cruise ship *Stockholm*. The *Stockholm*, left, with her ice-breaker bow stove in, has backed off and let down her lifeboats. The *Andrea Doria* is slowly on the way to the bottom with a gaping hole in her side.

To a Watery Grave

On the night of July 25, 1956, the fog off Nantucket was thicker than usual as the sleek Italian liner *Andrea Doria* rode gracefully over a gentle swell.

The pride of Italy's luxury fleet, under command of Capt. Piero Calamai, pushed steadily through the murky night as she headed for her New York City destination 200 miles away.

Five miles from the Doria, on an outbound course, was the trim, white-painted Swedish motorship *Stockholm.* She held to her course. So did the *Andrea Doria.*

At 11:20 P.M., the *Stockholm*'s graceful bow, heavily reinforced to fight ice in northern waters, tore a jagged hole in *Andrea Doria*'s starboard side just aft of the bridge. The hole was forty feet across at its widest point.

The *Stockholm*'s bow was folded back like a mashed tin can, but her wound was not mortal. Unfortunately, the *Doria*'s was, and almost immediately she began to list as tons of water poured into her gaping wound.

Maritime listening posts heard a chilling exchange of messages starting at 11:22 P.M.

11:22 (From the *Stockholm*): "We have collided with another ship. Please. Ship in collision."

11:25 (From the Coast Guard): "*Andrea Doria* and *Stockholm* collided. Latitude 40-30 North, Longitude 69-53 West."

11:30 (*Stockholm* to *Andrea Doria*): If you can lower lifeboats, we can pick you up."

11:35 (*Andrea Doria* to *Stockholm*): "We are bending (listing) . . . impossible . . . put lifeboats at sea . . . send immediate assistance . . . lifeboats."

Then about fifteen minutes later, the *Andrea Doria* sounded the dreaded SOS. Scores of craft, big and small, pointed their bows toward the area in which the Coast Guard reported the accident had occurred.

Fifty miles away, the great French liner, *Ile de France,* altered course as soon as the SOS was heard and sped at twenty-two knots through fog and arrived at the collision scene in under two hours.

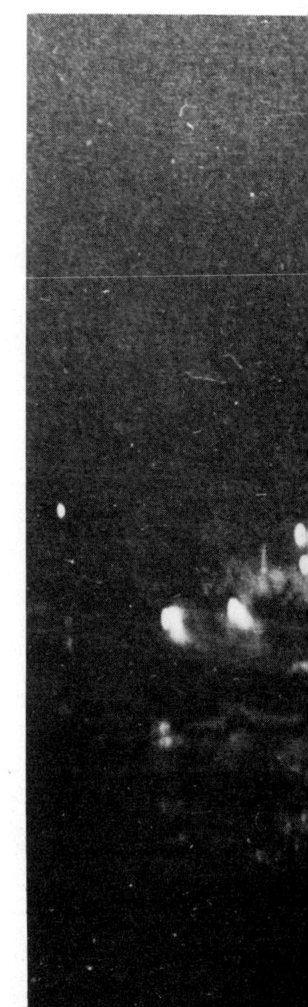

The *Andrea Doria* is listing badly with water up to her promenade deck. This photo was taken by a French Line photographer aboard the nearby *Ile de France.*

Meanwhile, on the *Doria,* passengers and crew started abandoning ship in orderly fashion. They either climbed down webbed rope ladders to waiting lifeboats, or simply slid down the oily side of the ship.

Across a quarter-mile of water, the lights of the *Ile de France* blazed brightly on the scene. More ships kept arriving, and more lifeboats plied back and forth until almost all of the *Doria*'s nearly 1,700 survivors had been taken off.

There were those who were never taken off. Fifty passengers—those who couldn't navigate the ladders or slide down the ship's side—were lost at sea.

At 4:48 A.M., the *Ile de France* would radio: "All passengers rescued. Proceeding to New York at full speed."

Shortly after 10 A.M., the pride of the Italian cruise fleet began to sink along her entire length. Under Navy escort, the *Stockholm* limped back to New York.

Millions of dollars in claims would be filed against both ship lines. But the burning question—which ship was responsible for the collision—was never answered.

For those fifty people who didn't survive the fatal collision, it didn't really matter.

A buoy tender stands by to take on a lifeboat filled with passengers from the listing *Andrea Doria*. The reflection in the photo in left center was halation from a plane window through which the picture was taken.

This dramatic closeup photo shows *Andrea Doria* listing heavily to starboard shortly before starting her fatal plunge to the ocean bottom off Nantucket.

This series of Coast Guard photos (continued on pages 68–69) shows the final moments of the Italian luxury liner as she rolls over and sinks beneath the waters. Only bubbles and debris remained as she disappeared beneath the surface.

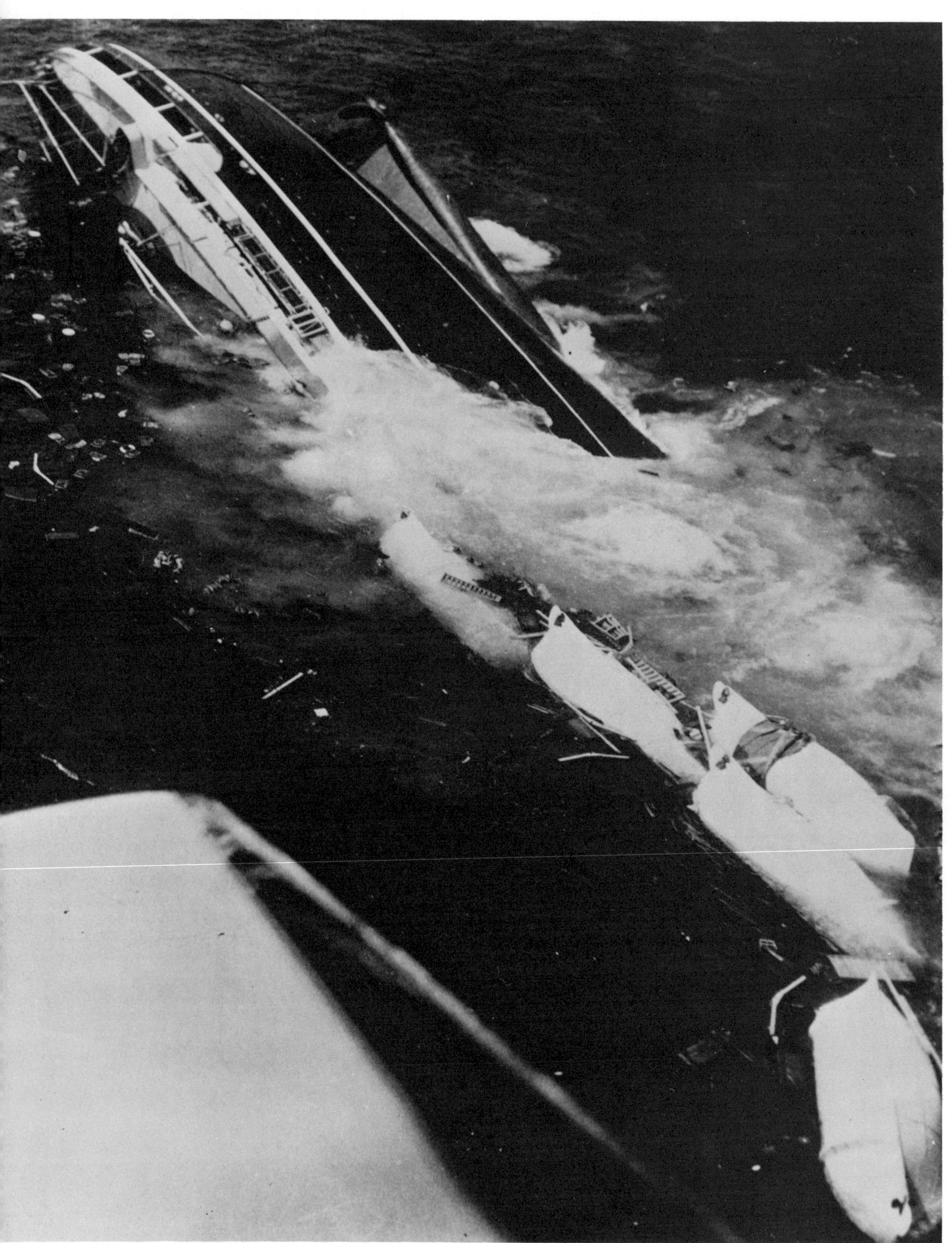

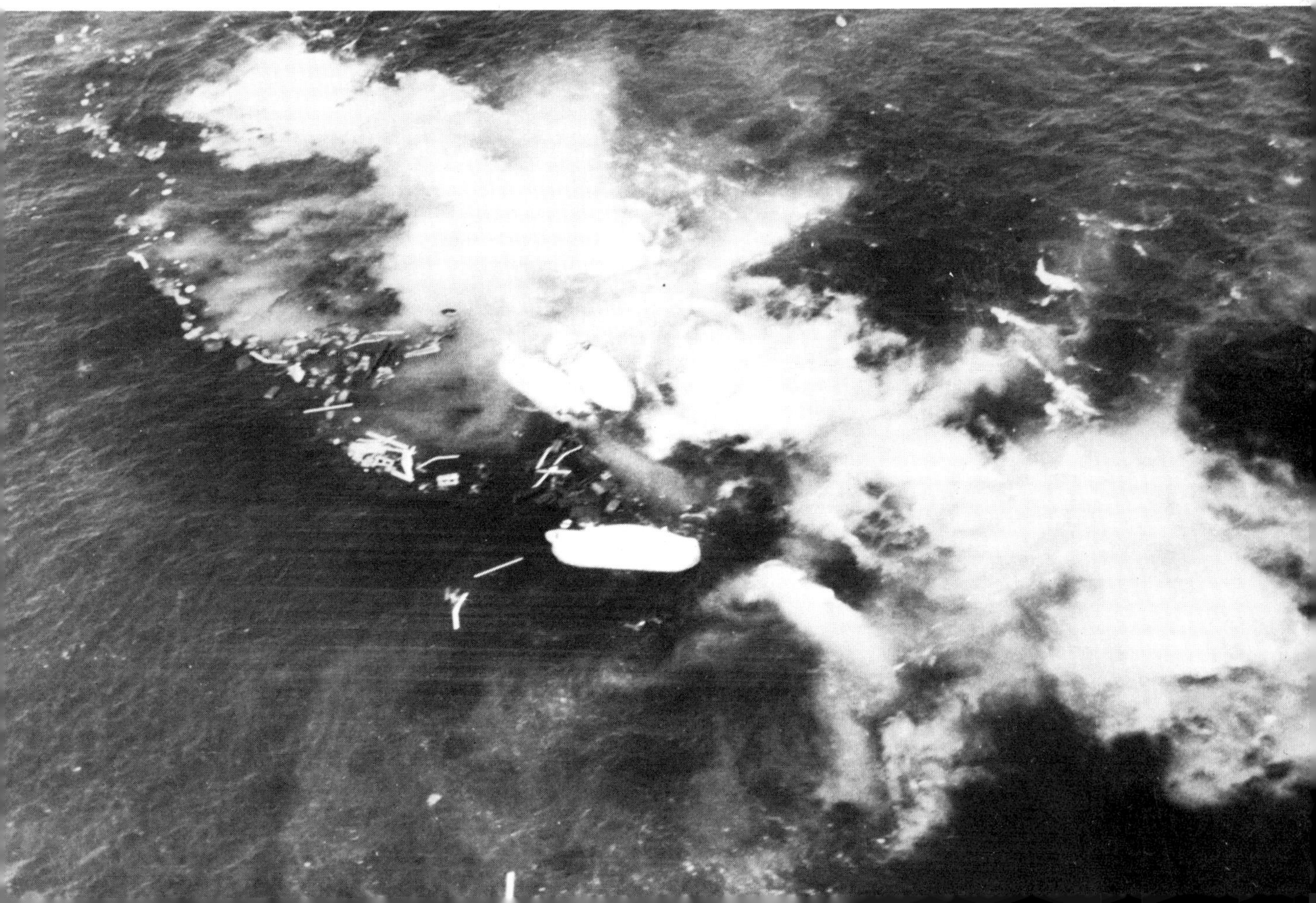

The captain and crewmen, who stayed with him almost to the end, head for rescue ships in lifeboats. Nearly all of *Andrea Doria*'s passengers and crew were rescued.

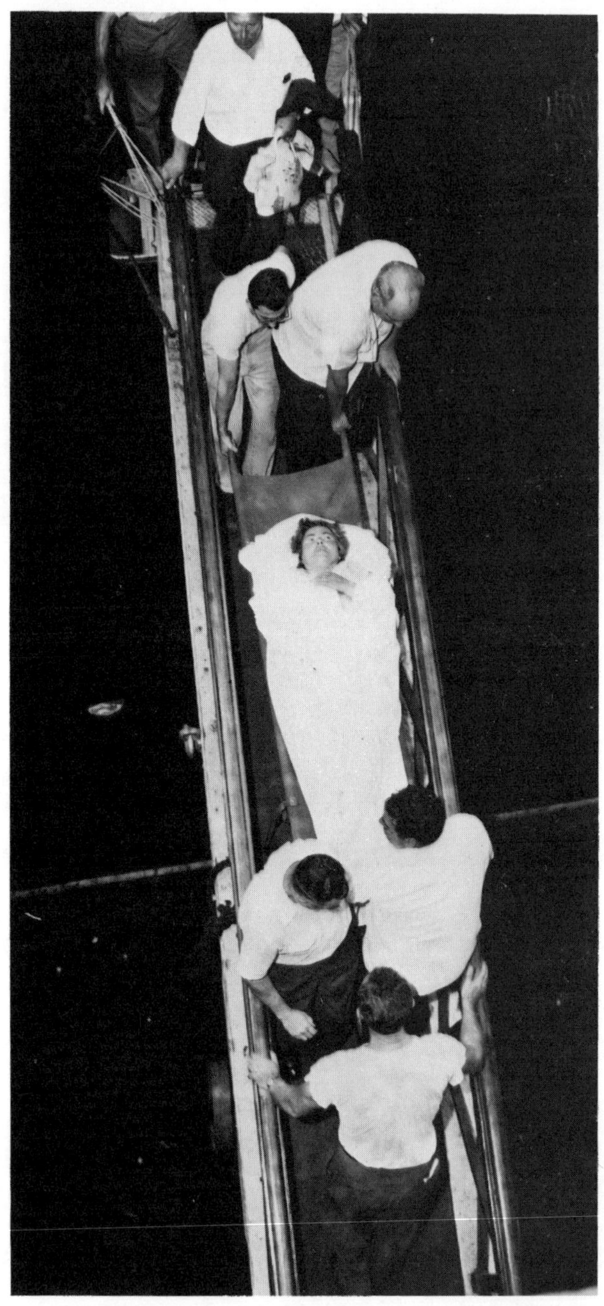

An unidentified woman on a stretcher is taken off the *Ile de France* after it arrived in New York with more than 700 survivors of the *Andrea Doria*.

Attempts at Salvage

Since the *Andrea Doria* went down on that fateful night of July 25, 1956, there have been several attempts to salvage her. As well there might be. The *Andrea Doria* was, after all, a luxury liner, and it had been estimated that there was some $2 million worth of treasure in money and valuables in the hull of the ship.

Various teams of would-be salvagers have been attracted to the site where the ship sank below the surface of the Atlantic Ocean, 45 miles south of Nantucket Island.

In 1963 a fathometer depth sounder aboard a salvage vessel graphed a view of the Italian liner. An electronic view of the wreck was made with a Raytheon depth sounder that sends out ultrasonic impulses and records echoes bouncing off the ocean's floor. It also records obstructions and passing fish. The fathometer recorded that the *Andrea Doria* lay 36 fathoms deep, or 216 feet beneath the sea's surface.

In 1971 two men constructed an 18-foot fiber glass and cement submarine in the hope that she

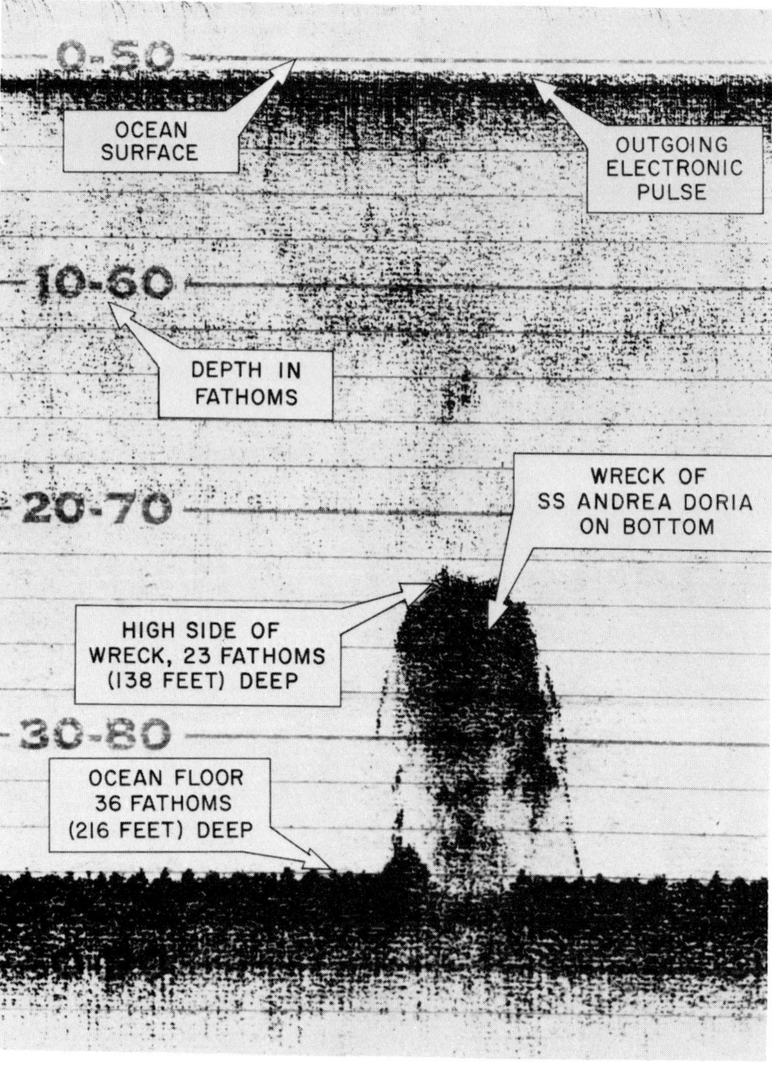

A reproduction of the fathometer depth sounder recordings indicating the "sound" of the sunken *Andrea Doria.*

would be seaworthy for their salvage operation on *Andrea Doria.* Their efforts came to naught.

A ten-day expedition led by three ex-Navy aquanauts took place in 1973. The underwater vessel that was home to them measured 5 feet by 12 feet. When the divers discovered that the hull was a massive tangle of broken rubble, the search was cut short. Various small items were found in a stateroom, but the treasure could not be reached.

Then in 1981 filmmaker Peter Gimbel launched a mammoth expedition to find the two safes that are believed to hold the *Andrea Doria*'s bounty. One two-ton safe was in fact recovered. It arrived in a water-filled box in Montauk Harbor and was then deposited and suspended in a tank filled with sharks at the New York Aquarium. The safe, safe-guarded by sharks, will remain sealed until it is opened as part of a television documentary Mr. Gimbel is preparing about the salvage operation.

Salvage Attempts

Michael Cushman, right, and Roger Frechette wave from the deck of their two-man submarine, *Scavenger.* Their salvage operation was to have taken place in 1971.

Divers prepare for their *Andrea Doria* salvage expedition in 1973.

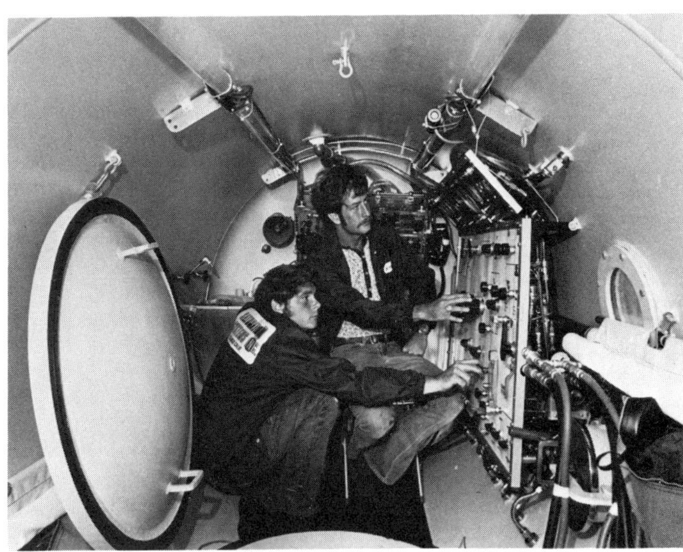

Ex-Navy Aquanauts Chris DeLucchi, left, and Don Rodocker check controls in the underwater vessel that is part of their exploration.

Crewmen haul in the underwater vessel when the ten-day expedition was cut short. As soon as the divers found the hull to be a tangle of broken rubble, the search was called off.

Divers Rodocker, left, and DeLucchi, step out of their *Habitat* in Fairhaven, Massachusetts. This salvage attempt to retrieve the purported $2 million in cash and other valuables was thwarted.

Master diver George Powell holds a bottle of perfume and a cover to a tray, two of the items recovered from a stateroom of the *Andrea Doria*.

The safe was brought to Montauk Harbor. A U.S. Customs chain and lock seals the Bank of Italy safe.

Filmmaker Peter Gimbel launched his salvage expedition in 1981. Here, workers aboard the *Sea Level II* hoist the one safe that was recovered.

Elga Anderson-Gimbel, wife of Peter Gimbel, sits atop the water-filled box that holds the safe. A member of the New York State Police stands guard.

The safe is suspended in the New York City Aquarium's shark tank until it is to be opened.

THE SIXTIES

Thresher

U.S.S. *Thresher*, pride of the Navy's nuclear submarine fleet, is shown during one of her sea trials. On April 9, 1963, while undergoing deep dive tests 220 miles east of Cape Cod, she sank with all hands in 8,400 feet of water.

Terror Beneath the Seas

The tragic loss of the *Thresher* is not unlike the drama of life and death played in the ocean depths nearly a quarter of a century earlier by the *Squalus*.

Thresher. She was the pride of the new U.S. underseas nuclear fleet. She boasted advanced navigation and underwater detection systems, vastly increased diving depth, and improved operating silence. She also was one of the fastest nuclear subs in the Navy.

Built nearly two years before, *Thresher* sailed out of its drydock at Portsmouth, New Hampshire, April 9, 1963, to undergo a series of deep-diving tests. Aboard were 129 men, some of them civilian engineers.

The naval operations log of the Atlantic Fleet tells part of the grim story:

Tuesday, April 9:

8:30 A.M. (EST)—*Thresher* proceeded to Boston operating area for rendezvous with Submarine Rescue Vessel *Skylark*.

11:00 A.M.—*Thresher* began initial dive in local Boston operating area in position where water depth was relatively shallow.

9:00 P.M.—*Thresher* successfully completed initial test trials and proceeded with *Skylark* to a spot approximately 220 miles east of Cape Cod to commence deep dives and remainder of sea trials.

Wednesday, April 10:

8:00 A.M.—*Thresher* and *Skylark* arrived at desired operating area. *Thresher* continued trials with *Skylark* standing by, maintaining sonar contact and underwater communication. All trials were successful at medium submerged depth. Deep dive trials were then commenced.

9:17 A.M.—Underwater communication between *Thresher* and *Skylark* became garbled and weak. *Skylark* continued to call *Thresher* by underwater telephone and sonar, but no further information was heard by *Skylark*.

At this point, the Navy reported, emergency surfacing signals were begun by *Skylark* in an attempt to reestablish underwater communication. When *Skylark* was unable to obtain a reply from *Thresher*, the commander of the Atlantic Fleet Submarine Force was notified and search operations were begun.

But all rescue operations would be in vain.

As *Thresher* dove to her maximum operating depth, the Navy later surmised, an engine room pipe carrying saltwater burst under the enormous pressures of depth and short-circuited the electrical system. With power gone, the submarine continued to sink until her pressure hull collapsed and settled her and her crew on the ocean floor, 8,400 feet deep.

Later, the deep-diving *Bathyscaphe Trieste II* would recover a small piece of tubing from the wreckage as well as take photographs of the remains, but the actual cause of the disaster would never be known.

Then Secretary of the Navy Fred Korth announced after a court of inquiry:

"The tragic loss of *Thresher* has caused the Navy to review in minute detail the design, construction, operation and overhaul of (all) our nuclear subma-

On July 8, 1961, the Portuguese steamer *Save* broke up in heavy seas off the Mozambique coast when a fire and explosion disabled the ship and left her adrift. The accident took 227 lives.

rines. We have found nothing to cast doubt on the basic soundness of the program. But in every analysis of major catastrophes at sea," he added, "lessons are learned."

An improvised buoy made of a red and white parachute holding inflated truck tires acts as a floating tombstone to mark the watery grave of *Thresher* and her crew. A smaller float attached to the buoy carries a light and radar reflector.

A big sea breaks against the port side of the research vessel *Atlantis II* as a breeches buoy is rigged to a nearby destroyer for transfer of sonar equipment to seek the grave of the missing nuclear sub.

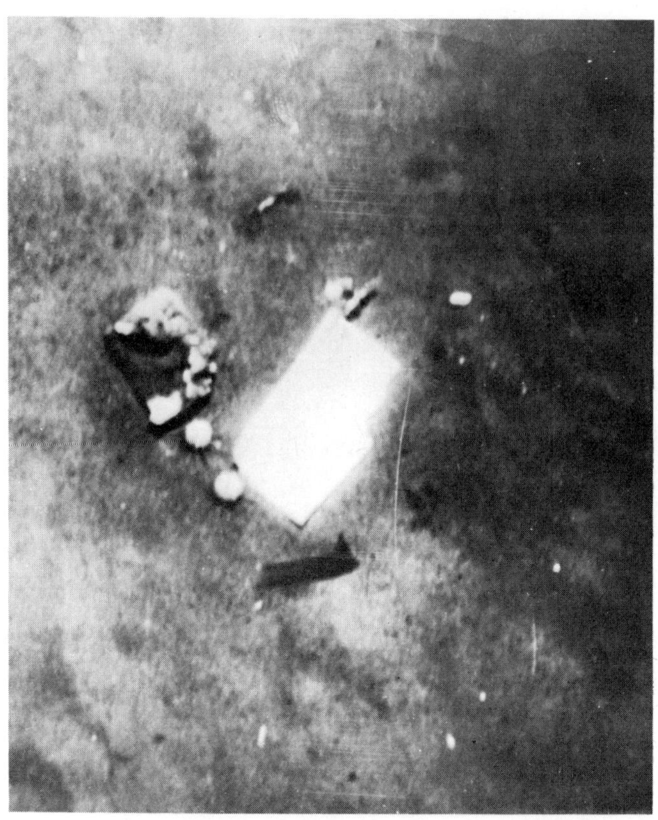

This Defense Department photo, taken 8,400 feet deep by cameras of *Atlantis II,* shows debris believed to mark the final resting place of *Thresher.*

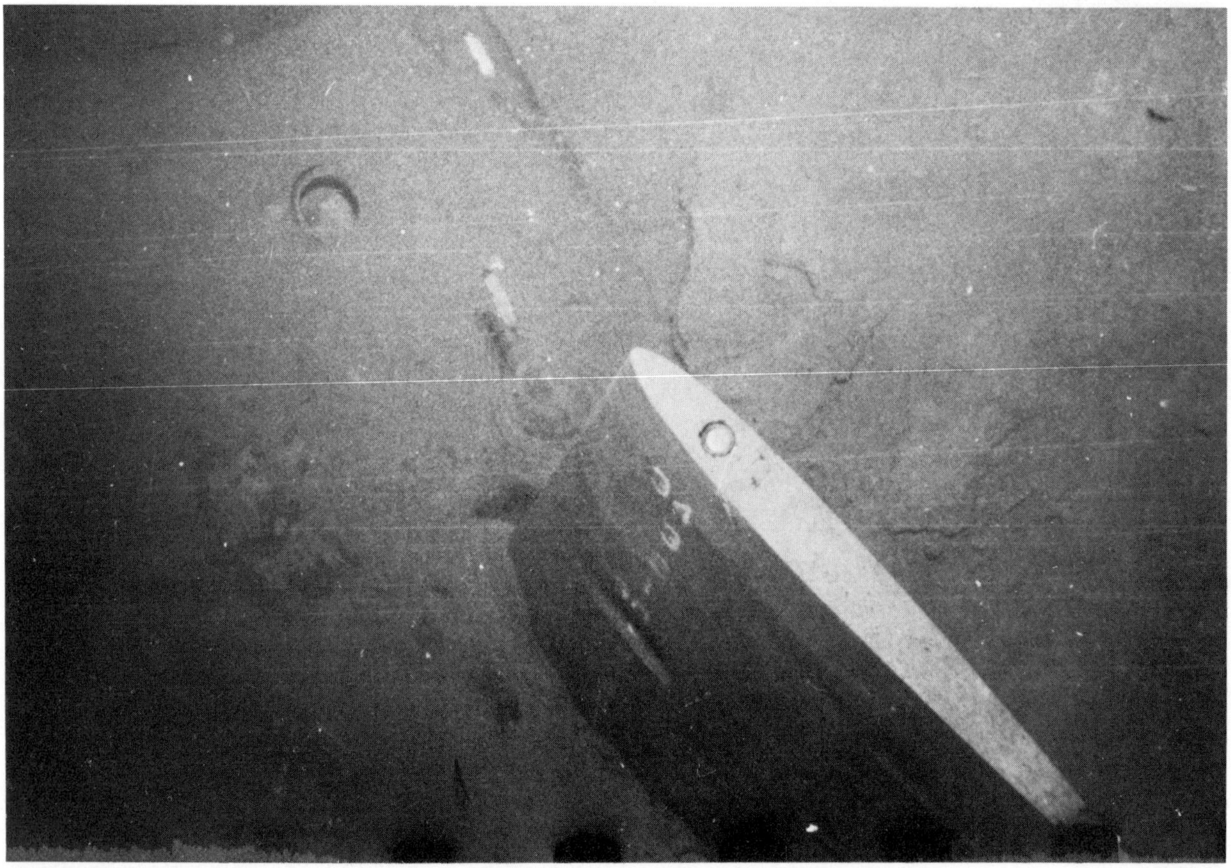

This photo, taken at a depth of more than 8,000 feet by the Navy's *Bathyscaphe Trieste II,* showed the top side of *Thresher*'s rudder.

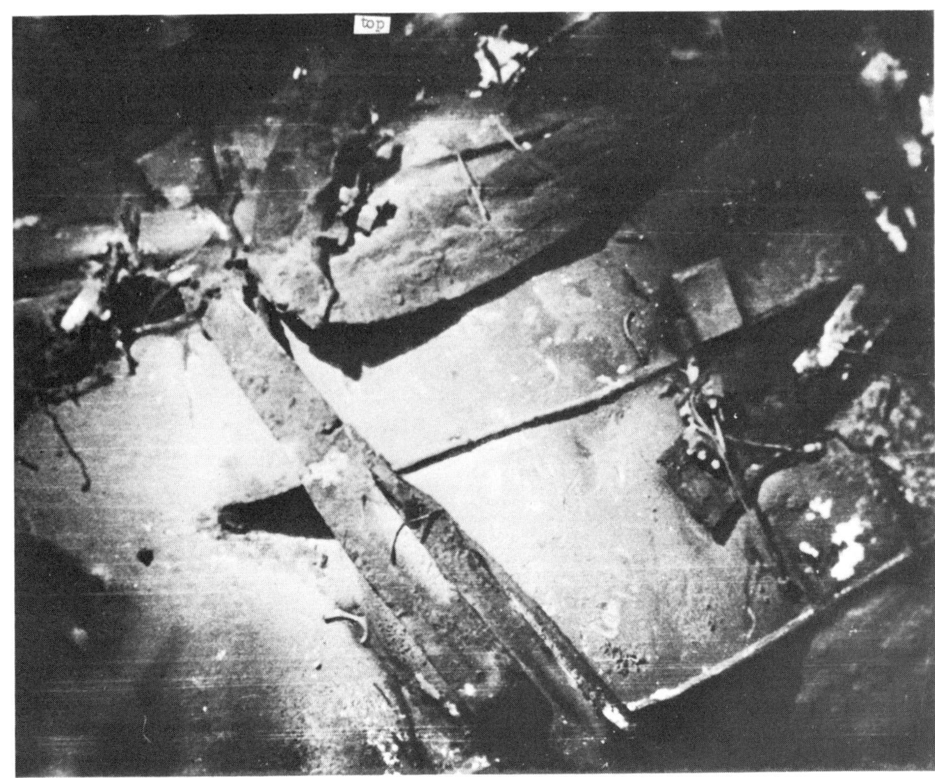

Additional wreckage located by the deep-diving *Bathyscaphe Trieste II* included the external portion of a sonar dome used exclusively in *Thresher*-type submarines.

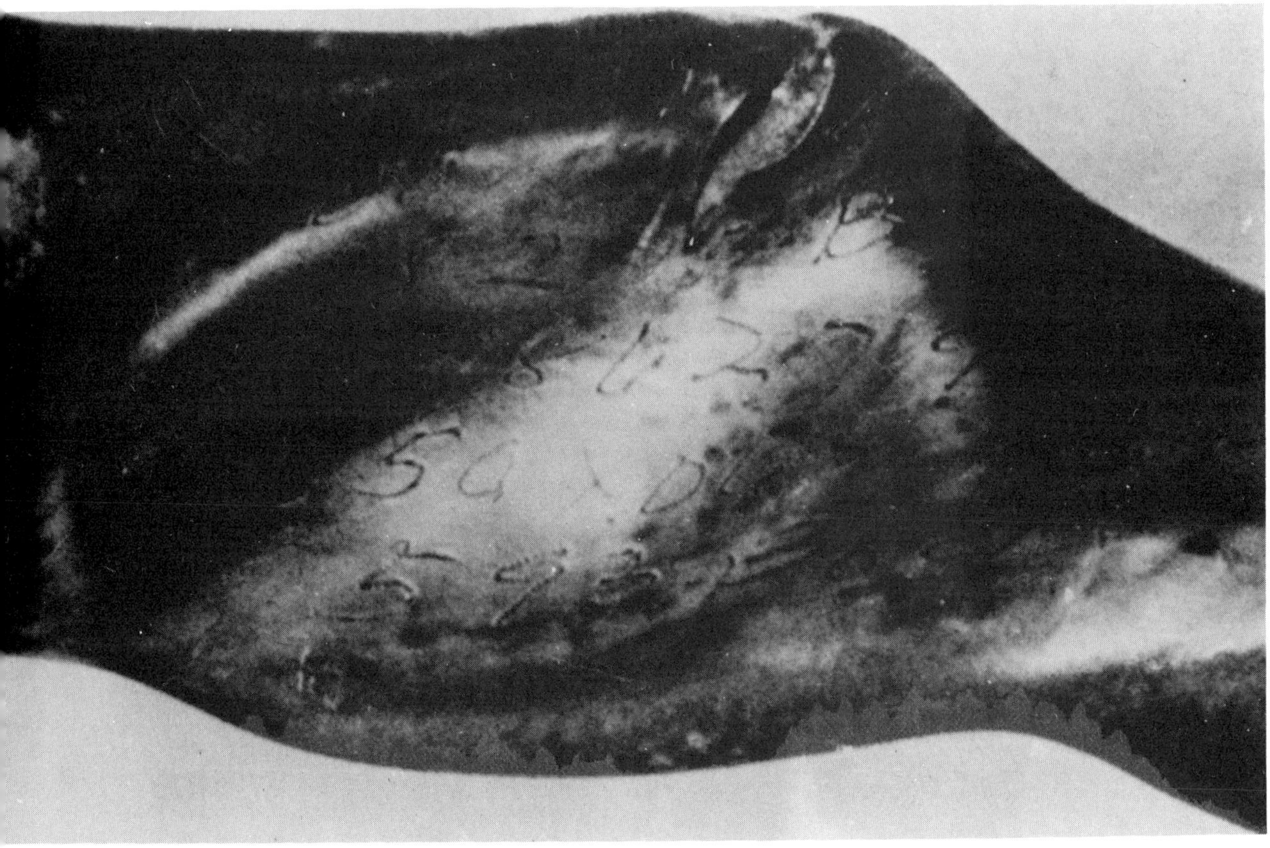

This section of a brass pipe photographed by *Trieste* contained the inscription, "593 Boat." The *Thresher*'s hull number was 593.

Bermuda Triangle

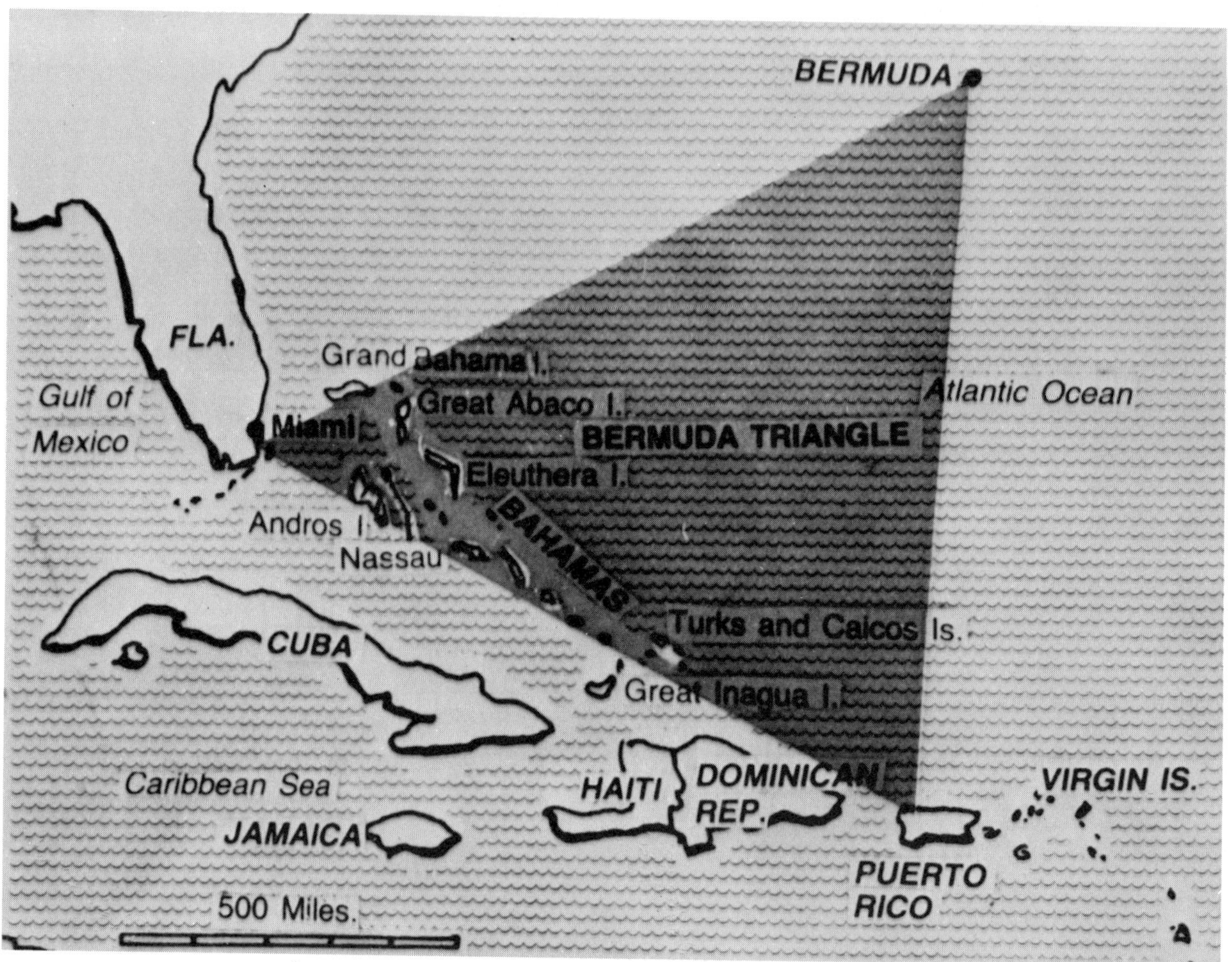

This map outlines the area of the Bermuda Triangle.

Swallowed at Sea

It is an area in the western Atlantic that extends from the island of Bermuda in the north to southern Florida, and then east to a point through the Bahamas past Puerto Rico to about 40 west longitude, and then back again to Bermuda. The area has sometimes been called "The Devil's Triangle," and more popularly, "The Bermuda Triangle." Since 1840 more than one hundred ships, and later, aircraft, have disappeared within this triangle. The great majority of these disappearances have occurred since 1945. More than one thousand lives have been lost to the sea. Ships, planes, people have vanished with hardly a trace. Studies and investigations have been conducted, findings reported, theories put forth, books written. One constant remains: the mysterious disappearances within the Bermuda Triangle continue to be just that—mysterious.

Consider the following events:

- The freighter, *Sandra,* sailed from Savannah, Georgia, for Venezuela with a crew of twelve and was never heard from.

- In 1918 the U.S. Navy supply ship, *Cyclops*, sailing from Rio de Janeiro to Baltimore, called at Barbados and proceeded into oblivion on March 4th. There were 309 people aboard the *Cyclops*. She disappeared without wiring a distress call.
- A plane departing from Puerto Rico carrying 32 people flew nearly 1,000 miles toward Miami, but never arrived.
- Having left Fort Lauderdale, Florida, five torpedo planes on a training flight never returned. A rescue plane with thirteen aboard was also lost.
- A British airliner, *Ariel*, departed from Bermuda for Chile, and simply vanished. There were twenty aboard.

Among these strange happenings, perhaps the most bizarre story is that of the tanker, *Sulphur Queen*. Loaded with liquid sulphur, she sailed from Beaumont, Texas, for Norfolk, Virginia, on February 2, 1963. *Sulphur Queen* was to have arrived in Norfolk on February 7. After having been sighted by another tanker on February 4 in the Dry Tortugas, she vanished completely. It was not until February 20 that two life jackets labeled S.S. *Marine Sulphur Queen*, a lifeboat foghorn, a sea marker, and several boxes were found in the Gulf of Mexico and brought to Miami, Florida. A life preserver tied to a man's shirt was also plucked from the sea. The helicopter crew said sharks surrounded the equipment when it was found in the water.

On December 22, 1963 the Greek liner, *Lakonia*, was en route to the Canary Islands and Madeira. The crew and passengers numbered 1,041 in all.

At about 11:00 P.M., Capt. M. N. Zarbis was alarmed to see a wall of fire emanating from the ship's barber shop toward the staterooms. Panic ensued, and although the amazing number of 18 boats helped in the rescue work, 155 lives were lost.

In the sometimes-forgotten tradition, Captain Zarbis was the last to abandon ship. The ill-fated *Lakonia* was then to be towed to Gilbraltar by two tugs, the *Herkules* and the *Polzee*. About 250 miles from their destination, the *Lakonia* suddenly went down in 2,000 fathoms. The precise cause of the fire will never be known.

(Opposite page) The supply ship *Cyclops* before it vanished in 1918 within the Bermuda Triangle, without wiring any distress calls. The Navy calls it one of the most baffling mysteries in her annals.

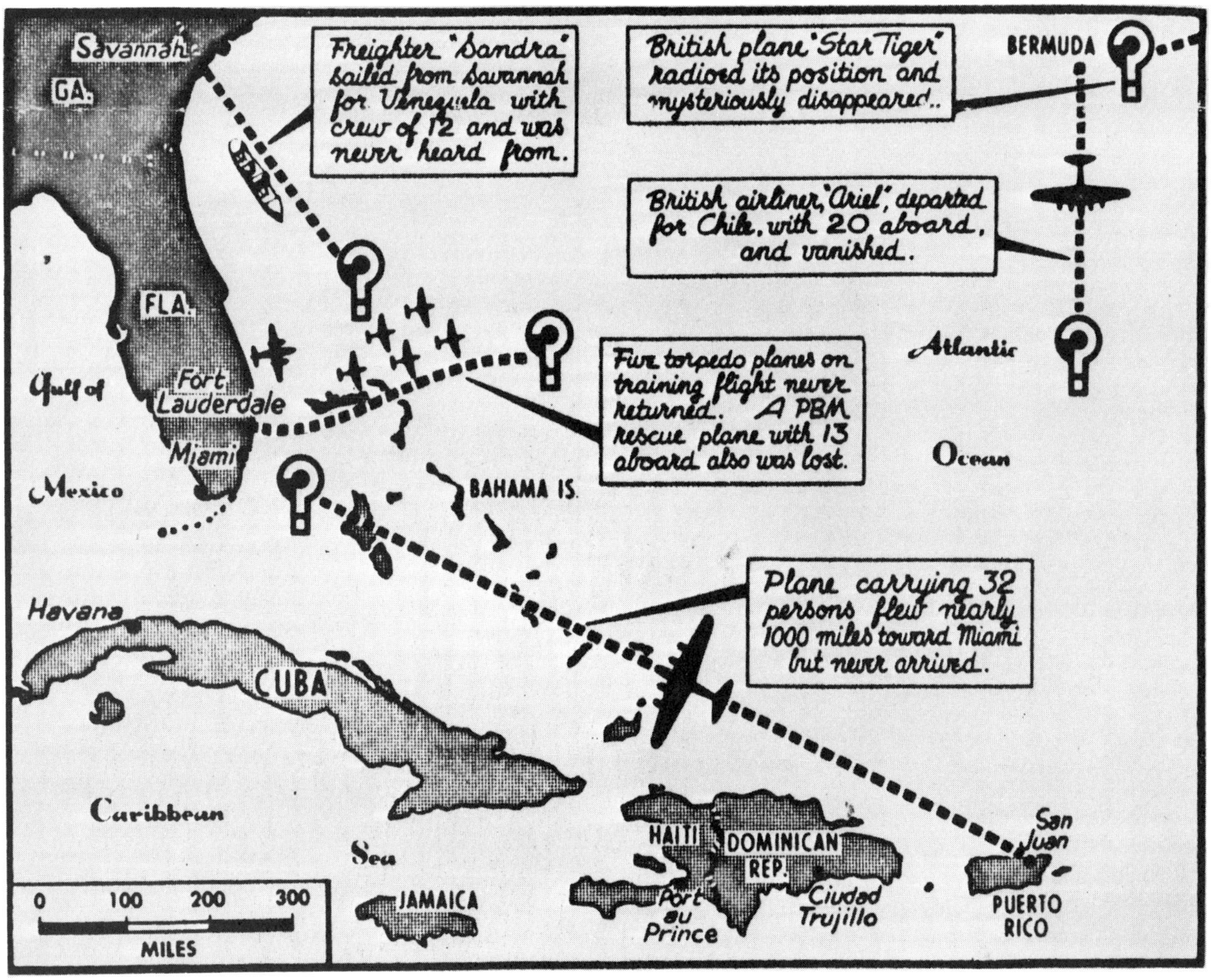

Five examples of mysterious events that took place are displayed in this map.

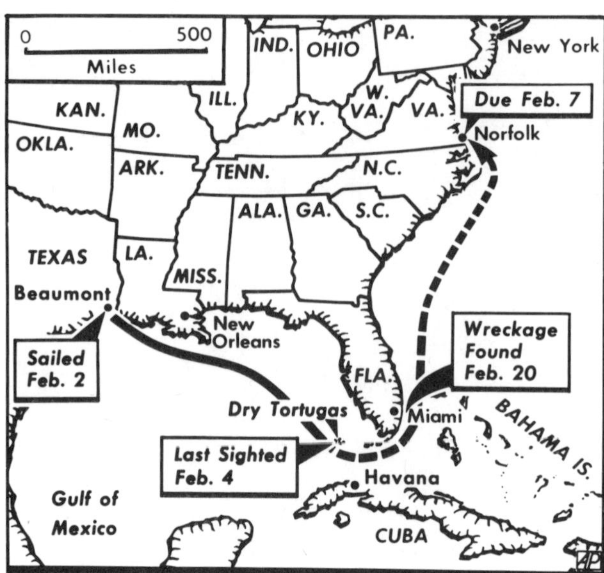

The aborted route of the tanker *Sulphur Queen* in February, 1963. The ship never reached her destination of Norfolk.

Among the flotsam discovered in the Gulf of Mexico, the Coast Guard found various items from the vanished tanker: a life preserver tied to a man's shirt, two life jackets, a lifeboat foghorn, a sea marker, and several boxes.

Cruise to Nowhere

Thanksgiving Day, 1964. Fighting high waves and heavy winds, the luxury liner *Shalom,* trim new flagship of Israel's Zim Lines, sliced through the fog-shrouded Atlantic about thrity-five miles off the New Jersey coast. On board were 616 Caribbean-bound passengers and a crew of 460.

The *Shalom*—her name meaning "peace" in Hebrew—had arrived in New York the previous May on her maiden voyage from her home port in Haifa. Built in France, the sleek, white $20-million liner had left her berth just a few hours before, after a series of gay, bon voyage parties aboard ship.

Her riding lights grew little haloes as she moved into an ever-increasing fog, and one by one her cabin portholes went dark as her passengers retired in the early morning hours.

The fog also was harassing another ship. She was the 12,723-ton Norwegian tanker *Stolt Dagali,* bound from Philadelphia to Newark, New Jersey, with a cargo of solvents and oil.

Shortly before 2:30 A.M., Coast Guard shore stations picked up the first distress call, apparently from the tanker.

The *Shalom*, steaming along in dense fog, had sliced into the Norwegian tanker and cut her in two. Both ships had been equipped with radar, but they apparently had not seen each other in time to avoid collision.

The bow of the much heavier liner had torn through the *Stolt Dagali*'s 70-foot width like a knife through butter. The stern section of the tanker quickly sank, taking nineteen seamen to their doom.

An aerial view of the Israeli luxury liner, the *Shalom*. More than 600 passengers and a crew of 460 were on board.

The *Shalom* sustained a 40-foot gash, four feet wide, just above the waterline, but the wound was not fatal. She would be able to limp back to her New York berth on her own power.

The master of the Norwegian tanker, Capt. Kristian Bendorsen, was on the bridge when the collision occurred.

"It was very foggy . . . we couldn't see," he testified later. He said the *Shalom* had split his ship completely in two and passed through it.

Immediately after the crash, he said, he sent out an SOS and then contacted the *Shalom* by radio and asked her to stand by and help.

Passengers on the Israeli ship said the collision produced no alarm or panic, although its force bowled over several late-night party-goers still on the dance floor. But it was a scene of horror on the *Stolt Dagali.*

In the instant, overwhelming confusion of the collision, some tanker survivors found themselves in the water, swimming for their lives, with no inkling of how they had gotten there—or why. Presumably, some of the victims trapped in the stern section of the tanker died without any realization of what happened.

Amid treacherous swells and heavy winds, the Coast Guard conducted a massive air-and-sea rescue. A short time after picking up the distress calls, rescue planes were already dropping magnesium flares above the collision scene. But fog had all but smothered their glare.

Those survivors who were later picked up by surface vessels and helicopters were oil-smeared, blue with cold and, in some cases, temporarily insensible from shock.

In all, twenty-four crew members from the tanker—including a woman stewardess—were plucked from the raging seas or from the remains of the stricken ship. And in the true tradition of the sea, her exhausted and saddened skipper, Bendorsen, was the last to leave.

In the first light of the icy morning, only debris etched a grim reminder of the tragedy along a five-mile stretch of angry ocean.

Shalom

After having sliced the Norwegian tanker *Stolt Degali* in two in a pre-dawn collision off the New Jersey coast, the *Shalom* heads for New York harbor.

These pictures show the *Shalom*'s bow damaged just above the water line. Having been torn through, the *Stolt Dagali*'s stern section quickly sank. Nineteen seamen died.

Yarmouth Castle

Flames, reflected on the quiet sea, light up the night sky as the *Yarmouth Castle* burns some 100 miles east of Miami. The 365-foot cruise ship, en route to Nassau in the Bahamas, sank with a loss of 90 passengers and crew.

A Living Hell

She was built in Philadelphia in 1926 and put into service as the *Evangeline* the following year—one of two flagships of the Eastern Steamship Lines on the Boston to Nova Scotia summer run.

During World War II, she served as a troop carrier, then later as a carrier that brought thousands of war brides back to the United States.

But in 1964, a Panamanian steamship company ignored an old seaman's tale—that it was bad luck to change the name of a ship—and rechristened the *Evangeline* as the *Yarmouth Castle*. Almost immediately, the 365-foot vessel encountered ill fortune. Twice she left Bahama-bound passengers stranded on New York piers. Once she broke her moorings and rammed another ship. Often, she failed to meet scheduled speed.

Then, in the early morning hours of November 13, 1965, as *Yarmouth Castle* steamed 110 miles east of Miami on a cruise to Nassau, she encountered her worst piece of luck. Just after 1:00 A.M., fire broke out in what was believed to be an unoccupied stateroom in the forward part of the ship.

Within moments, flames licked upward to the radio shack, and billows of smoke cascaded up the stairwells as the blaze engulfed one deck after another.

Twenty-two-year-old passenger Terrill Eliseusen, one of the 375 vacationers aboard *Yarmouth Castle,* was awakened by the sound of shouting. "I opened the door of our cabin, but the hall was full of smoke. You couldn't see a thing . . . I smashed the porthole with my fist. It was the only way to get out. It was either that or stay and die." Another passenger, Joyce Paluch, described the scene as a "living hell."

Then, recalled Capt. Byron Vatsounas, "the upper deck split open like a flaming crater." Terrified passengers inched out of their cabins and scrambled for lifeboats. The decks were bedlam; pajama-clad passengers leaped into the ocean in fright. Said one survivor: "Those who hesitated just didn't make it."

In all, 90 passengers and crew didn't make it. Some suffocated in the halls; others burned to death. More than 450 were rescued by two nearby cruiseships.

Shortly after 6:00 A.M., while the survivors and rescuers watched in silence, the 38-year-old ship, aflame in the dawn, listed slightly to port. Then she suddenly heeled over and sank. "It was like the end of a nightmare," remarked Capt. John Leido of the *Finnpulp.*

Once safely delivered to Nassau, many passengers criticized the *Yarmouth Castle* (which did not fly an American flag and so was not subject to U.S. Maritime rules) for negligence.

One passenger, Gerald McDonnell of Silver Springs, Maryland, angrily declared: "I think it's a disgrace. They didn't have any life preservers in the cabin. The ropes had been painted and they couldn't lower the boats. There were no life rings on deck. We had no fire drill. We didn't have any warning. The regular alarm didn't go off and the overhead sprinkler didn't work either."

There are dozens of shipwrecks whose disasters can never be fully explained. One such case is that of the giant dredge, *Kaptajn Nielsen.* On September 18, 1964, she inexplicably capsized and sank to the bottom of Australia's Brisbane Harbor. Thirty-three men were fatally imprisoned at the bottom of the sea, although 15 crew did manage to escape. They, too, seemed unable to describe what exactly had happened to the dredge.

This is a closeup of the blaze, believed to have started in an unoccupied stateroom in the forward section of the ship.

Some of the survivors of the one-time World War II troop carrier approach the rescue boat *Bahama Star* by lifeboat.

A Coast Guard helicopter prepares to land on *Bahama Star* to take some of the *Yarmouth Castle*'s injured passengers to a hospital in Nassau.

An unidentified survivor of the *Yarmouth Castle* fire heads for a hospital in the Miami area. He was one of the more seriously injured in the sea disaster.

Smoke markers indicate the site where the burning *Yarmouth Castle* plunged to a watery grave. The ship in foreground is the *Bahama Star* which picked up the majority of passengers and crew from the ship.

The cruise ship *Bahama Star* drops anchor at Nassau, carrying the 367 survivors of the *Yarmouth Castle.*

Scorpion

The U.S.S. *Scorpion,* the Navy's atomic-powered submarine. Vice Adm. Hyman G. Rickover stands at left on diving plane with Cmdr. James F. Calvert.

Final Mission

The U.S.S. *Scorpion* was one of the deadliest weapons in the Navy's underwater arsenal. Commissioned in July of 1960 as one of six attack submarines in the Skipjack class at a cost of $40 million, she displaced more than 3,000 tons over a length of 252 feet.

Her nuclear engines gave her an operating range of some 60,000 miles without refueling and could drive her at a speed of up to thirty-five knots beneath the ocean surfaces. *Scorpion*'s sting was twenty-four torpedoes which she could fire at targets through six forward tubes.

In 1962, she received a measure of fame by setting an endurance record of seventy consecutive days beneath the surface.

Six years later, on May 27, 1968, the *Scorpion* would again make headlines.

Scorpion was homeward-bound after extensive maneuvers in the Mediterranean, and had surfaced at midnight on May 21 about 250 miles south of the Azores to radio her position to Norfolk, Virginia. It would be the last message anyone would hear from the sub or her ninety-nine-man crew.

A deadly weapon in the Navy's underwater arsenal, the *Scorpion*'s nuclear engines gave her an operating range of some 60,000 miles without refueling and a speed of up to 35 knots beneath the sea.

The sleek vessel should have reported in by midday of the 27th as she approached Norfolk. When she didn't, the Navy immediately launched a massive search along the route *Scorpion* would have taken from the area of her last radio message.

At the time, Navy officials speculated that the *Scorpion* might have chosen to ride out severe Atlantic weather by remaining submerged. They also suggested that in bad weather a message informing Norfolk she was being delayed could have been lost.

But Navy officials also acknowledged that the submarine would have attempted to contact shore by a number of other signals in the event her radio communications failed.

More than fifty naval vessels fanned out across the Atlantic in an attempt to discover the fate of *Scorpion.* And as the rescue effort stretched from days into weeks, hopes soon dimmed that some traces of the missing ship or crew would be found.

Early in the rescue effort, Mr. and Mrs. Howard Lloyd of Joliet, Illinois, parents of the sub's executive officer, Lt. Cmdr. David Lloyd, 33, said they hadn't given up hope but felt that the *Scorpion* "might be on the bottom of the sea."

It was not until many months later—in late October—that the mystery of *Scorpion*'s disappearance was solved.

While making measurements of the ocean bottom about 400 miles southwest of the Azores, the naval oceanographic research ship *Mizar* picked up something on her metal detectors in about 10,000 feet of water. On October 30, deep-reading cameras confirmed the worst: the wreckage lying on the ocean bottom was, indeed, the remains of the *Scorpion.*

But what the cameras didn't answer is exactly what had doomed the *Scorpion.* Speculation ranged widely.

The lone survivor of *Scorpion*'s crew, Communications Technician Joseph Underwood, had been put to shore at Rota, Spain, because of a possible lung infection. He would testify later that the sub had lost a lot of hydraulic fluid from a leaking periscope fitting before he left her.

And some oceanographers speculated that *Scorpion* might have been the victim of an "underwater wave" that plunged her far below her safe operating depth.

Still others felt that she might have been accidentally rammed by a Russian destroyer which had been spotted in the area.

All this was speculative thinking. The truth lies on the bottom of the Atlantic—along with the remains of ship and crew.

The Australian aircraft carrier *Melbourne* appeared to be a jinxed ship. On June 2, 1969, while on battle duty off the South Vietnamese coast, *Melbourne* struck the U.S. destroyer *Frank E. Evans* and killed 74 crewmen. Five years earlier, she had struck the Australian destroyer *Voyager* in Jervis Bay, New South Wales, and sank it along with 82 of its crew.

By May 27, 1968, the *Scorpion* had not been heard from and the Navy launched a massive search. Here Lt. Cmdr. Al Stetz, left, briefs his flight crew at Norfolk Naval Air Station before taking off to find the missing sub.

Robert P. Violetti, 21 year-old torpedoman, who was aboard the *Scorpion*. Before the sub was reported missing, he wrote to his mother, Mrs. Luella A. Violetti, saying that a Soviet destroyer had followed the *Scorpion* in the eastern Mediterranean on May 10, 1968.

Crew members of a Navy P-2 Neptune search aircraft search the Radar Scope and sounding devices as they fly a search pattern some 80 miles off the coast of Virginia.

The oceanographic research vessel, U.S.N.S. *Mizar,* used this sea bottom detector to locate the *Scorpion* in about 10,000 feet of water, some 400 miles southwest of the Azores. Standing, left to right: Capt. James D. Hobbs of Mizar, Rear Adm. Walter F. Schech, Jr., and Chester A. Buchanan.

In January 1969, the Department of Defense released this series of photographs of various parts of *Scorpion* resting on the bottom of the ocean floor:

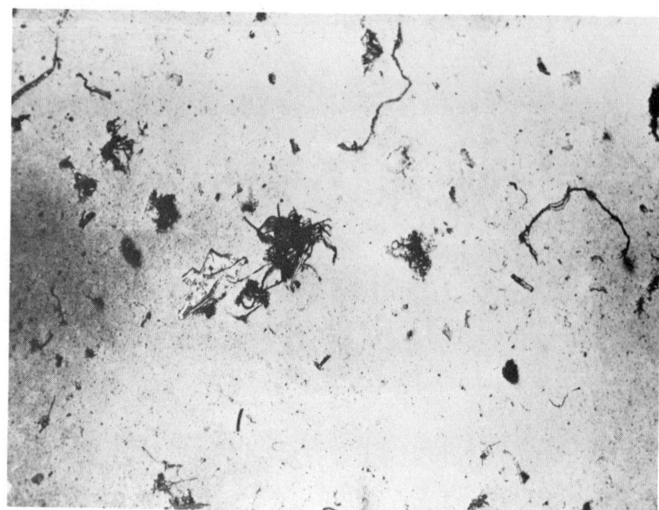

Debris found near the sub.

A view of *Scorpion*'s bow section.

The after section of the vessel where the messenger buoy is stored. A mooring line protrudes from its storage locker into the buoy cavity.

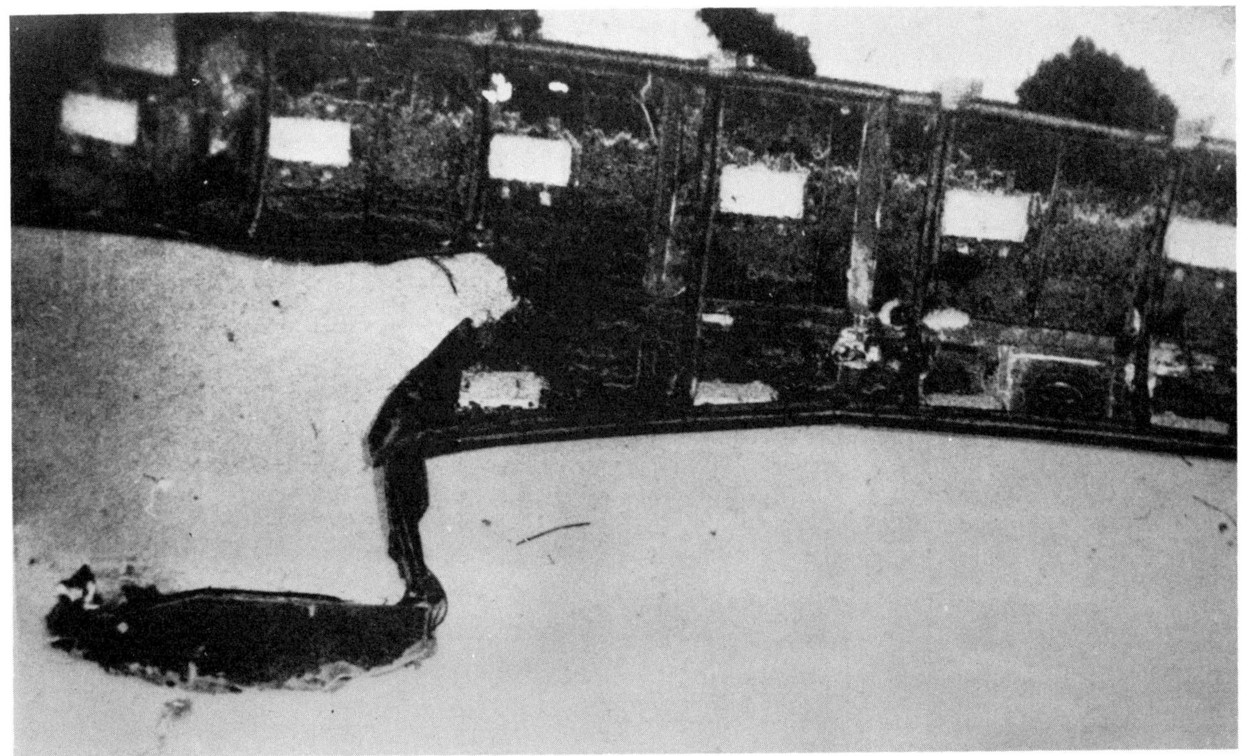

A damaged section of *Scorpion*'s snorkel exhaust piping fairing.

The access door from the port side of the sail of the submarine.

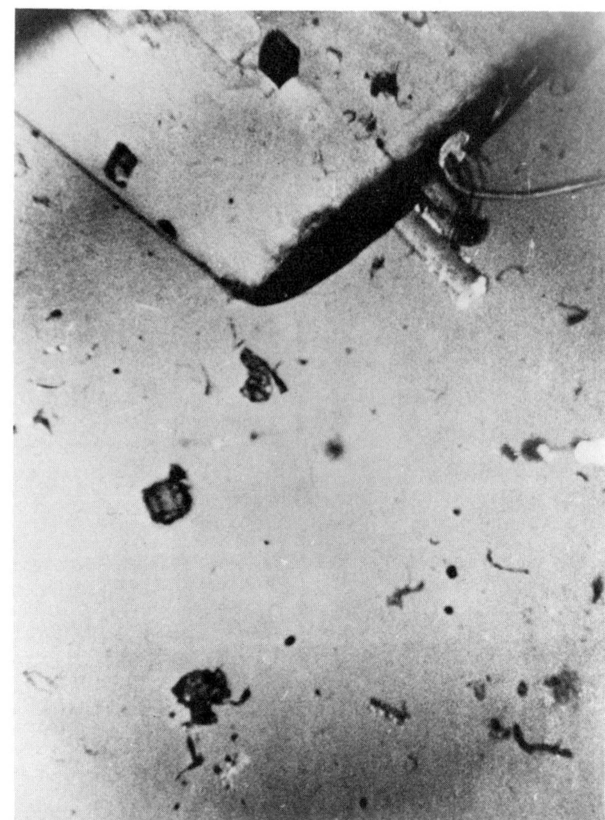

Part of *Scorpion*'s sail.

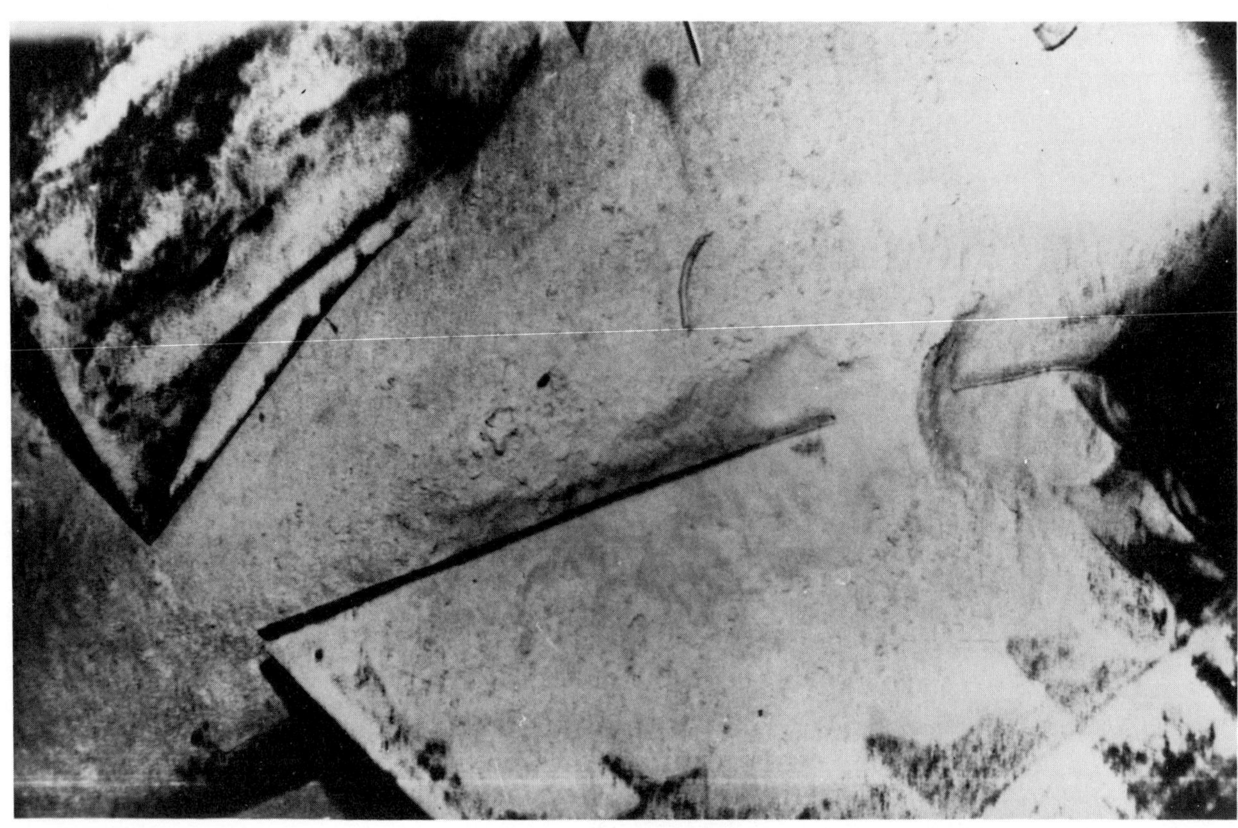

A stern view of *Scorpion* showing a portion of the rudder in the lower right and a portion of the stern plane in the upper left.

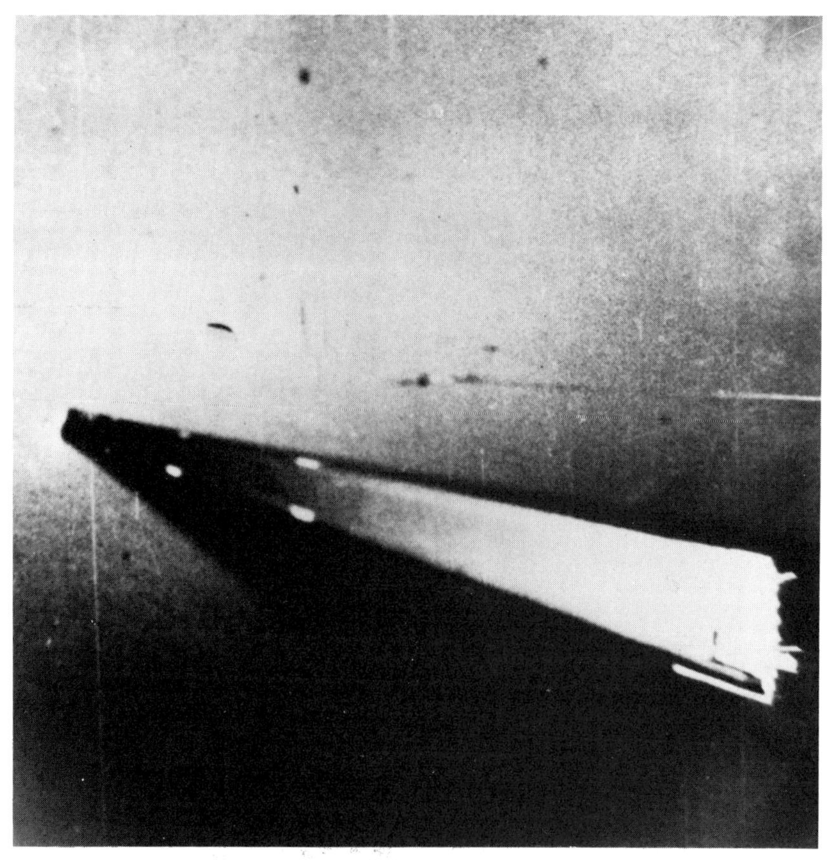

An antenna from the sub that is embedded in the ocean floor.

The starboard side of the sunken *Scorpion.* A door is visible at center. At top center are the periscope fairing and masts protruding from the sail. The white portion area is the area the Department of Defense said was not photographed in this mosaic.

THE SEVENTIES

A Korean Incident

On the afternoon of Dec. 15, 1970, the 362-ton ferry *Namyung Ho* left Cheju Island off Korea's southeast coast bound for the port city of Pusan. On board were 335 people, including 16 crewmen, and an estimated 400–500 tons of cargo—a heavier than normal load for a boat this size.

At 2:00 A.M. the following day, the *Namyung Ho* was located in the Korean Straits about 80 miles southwest of Pusan when the engines suddenly stopped.

A 55-year-old woman passenger, Choi Ok-Wa, would testify later that after the engines had stopped, the boat continued to drift powerless for about an hour. Suddenly, she said, the ferry started to list to port and then capsized.

Choi Ok-Wa was one of only 12 survivors, most of whom were plucked from the icy seas by Japanese fishing boats. Three U.S. Air Force planes, as well as Korean Air Force and police planes were enlisted in the search, which was called off when darkness fell. Korean skin divers were able to recover only nine bodies.

Like the Bermuda Triangle, America's Great Lakes have their own legends of mysterious ship disappearances. One of these mysteries concerns the ore carrier *Edmund Fitzgerald,* immortalized in a Gordon Lightfoot ballad. The 729-foot ship apparently broke apart and sank during a storm on Lake Superior on November 10, 1975. All 29 crewmen perished and only one empty wooden lifeboat and two rubber rafts were found floating on the icy lake two days later.

The Korean police blamed the incident on overloading. They arrested the boat's skipper as well as five others in connection with the sinking.

Kang Tae Soo, the 53-year-old captain of the *Namyung Ho;* Kang Woo Chin, its owner; and radioman Kim Bak Chi, all were charged with homicide and negligence of duty. Three port officials were also charged with negligence.

Less than a month later, another South Korean ferry, the *Kilja-Ho,* went down off the south coast with a loss of 35 lives after it collided with a 60-ton fishing boat. The ferry, carrying about 90 passengers and crew, was en route to Yosu from Gaeda Island, twelve miles offshore, and went down about 300 yards out. Fortunately, two police boats were able to rescue most of the passengers and six crewmen.

A Japanese fishing boat searches for survivors of the *Namyung Ho.* The debris in the photograph's foreground is believed to be part of the capsized ferry.

Namyung Ho

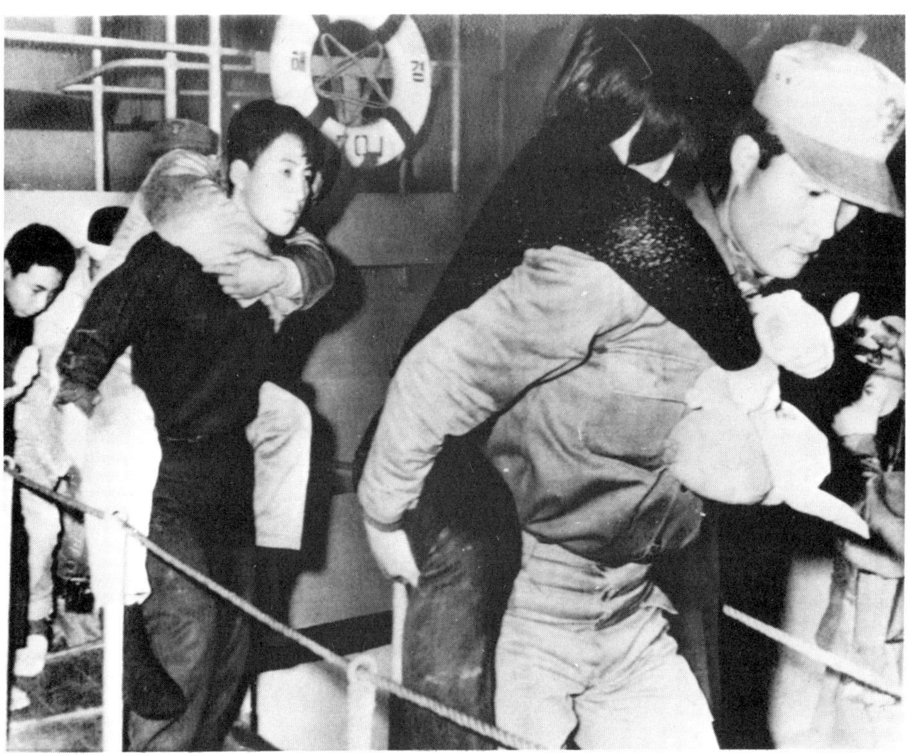

Only twelve people survived the *Namyung Ho* disaster. Here survivors are carried piggyback style or walked off a rescue vessel on arrival in Pusan, South Korea.

Two women survivors (top) and the *Namyung Ho*'s captain, Kang Woo Chin, cling to floating planks after the ferry sank. Kang Woo Chin was subsequently charged with homicide and negligence of duty.

River of No Return

The winds were brisk and chilly as the Mississippi River ferry *George Prince* left its berth at Destrehan, Louisiana, located twenty miles upriver from New Orleans. In the half-light of dawn on October 20, 1976, she was carrying ninety-six sleepy-eyed passengers on a ten-minute trip across the river to Luling, where most of them worked.

Most of the passengers who drove cars or trucks onto the 120-foot ferry stayed in them, windows rolled up to protect them against the chill. Other walk-on passengers stayed within the warm main cabin.

As the *George Prince* made her way across river, the 664-foot Norwegian tanker *Frosta* steamed slowly up the Mississippi, headed for a Baton Rouge oil refinery to load. Capt. Kjell Slatten was in his cabin near the bridge; river pilot N. S. Columbo had the helm. Under normal circumstances, a ferry yields the right-of-way to larger, less maneuverable ships using the main channel.

The *Frosta* spotted the ferry and gave it two warning whistles, a signal directing an oncoming vessel to pass on the right side. By the time Captain

If horse racing is the sport of kings, then yacht racing is the sport of princes, and one of the more prestigious events in the world of yachting is the Fastnet Race—a 670-mile track from the Isle of Wight in the English Channel to southern Ireland and return. In August of 1979, a flotilla of 306 yachts sailed out in less than ideal conditions. On the return leg, gale force winds and mountainous seas battered the small craft. Twenty-one boats sank and 17 yachtsmen drowned in what is called the worst disaster in yachting history. Among the survivors was Ted Turner, owner of the Atlanta Braves and the 1977 America's Cup victor.

The Norwegian tanker *Frosta* rides anchor upstream from Luling, Louisiana, after colliding with the Mississippi River ferry *George Prince*. The ferry sank with a loss of 78 lives, but little damage is visible on the tanker.

Slatten got to the bridge, the pilot was sounding a four-whistle alarm, the river signal for danger.

Captain Slatten would testify later that the ferry never changed course or speed when the tanker rammed the *George Prince* amidships and flipped it over like a toy.

Some of the thirty-five vehicles thrown off the ferry deck by the impact floated a few seconds, then sank slowly into the murk of the muddy river. The bodies of others, including those of the *George Prince*'s Capt. Egidio Auletta and his crew, would be recovered later from the hulk of the ferry.

In all, seventy-eight people aboard the ferry perished in what was described as one of the worst maritime accidents on the Mississippi in a century.

Several ferry survivors said the engines of the *George Prince* had stopped shortly before the crash, but no one knew why the collision occurred.

But an autopsy was performed on Captain Auletta, and the New Orleans coroner would report that the skipper was "almost legally drunk, and this coupled with the fact that he was at the end of his shift . . . in my judgment impaired his judgment and ability to handle his vessel."

Rescuers check the bow section of the *George Prince* after she was rammed by a tanker and capsized. The ferry, loaded with passengers and cars, was hit amidships during the half light of dawn.

George Prince

Rescue workers huddle under blankets as the search for bodies continues on the Mississippi River at Luling, Louisiana.

A motorcycle that was on the ferry *George Prince* is hauled from the river bottom. Many of the victims had been sitting in their cars when the accident occurred.

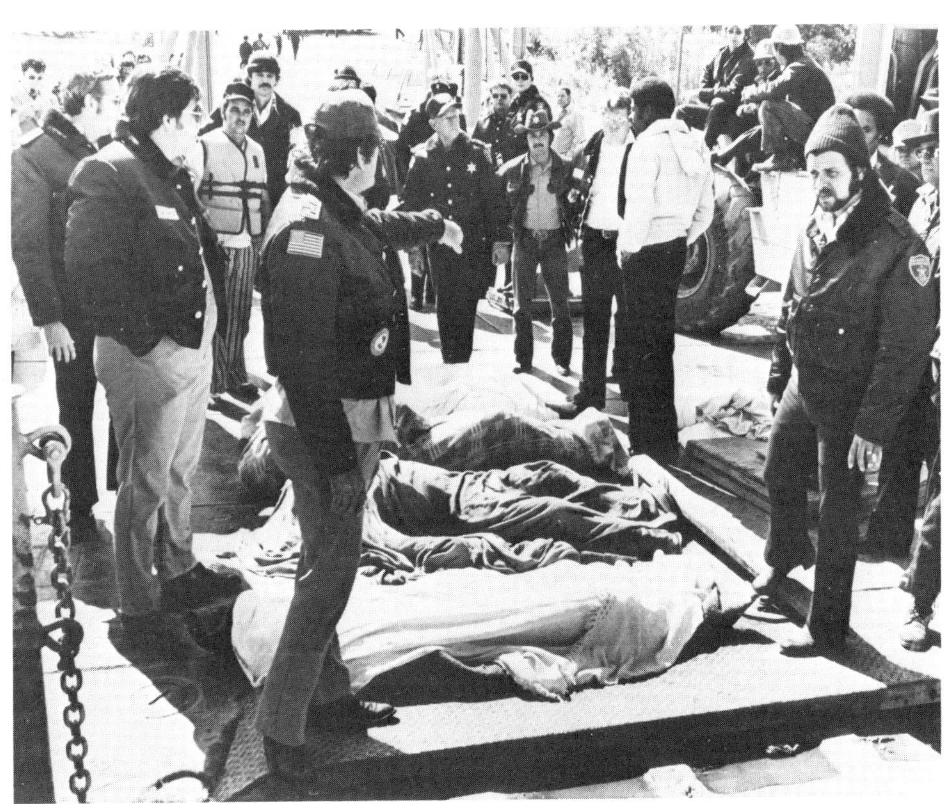

Deputies and rescue workers stand around covered bodies recovered from the river. Most of the victims were headed to the refineries and plants at Luling, a ten-minute crossing from Destrehan, Louisiana.

Some of the cars and trucks that were on board the ferry sit in their own graveyard after they were pulled from the river.

Mrs. Egidio Auletta, wife of the skipper of the ferry *George Prince,* sits in a small boat as she awaits word on the fate of her husband. His body was later recovered from the water.

Mute testimony to the tragedy: a worker's lunch pail is fished from the river by one of the rescuers.

Four victims of the ferry-tanker collision lie covered on the banks of the Mississippi at Luling. In background is the ferry *Ollie K. Wilds,* sister ship of the *George Prince.*

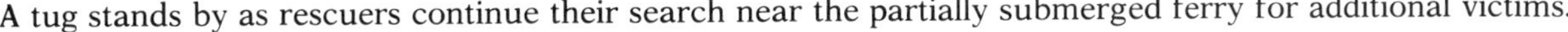

A tug stands by as rescuers continue their search near the partially submerged ferry for additional victims.

A man holds an oar that washed ashore from the *George Prince.* A portion of the bow of the ferry projects from the waters of the Mississippi River.

The ferry *George Prince* is finally raised, and is boarded by inspectors before it is towed away.

Chronology of Twentieth-Century Shipwrecks

1. *General Slocum,* New York City, 1904
2. *Norge,* Scotland, 1904
3. *Principe de Asturias,* off Spain, 1912
4. *Titanic,* North Atlantic, 1912
5. *Kichemary,* off Japan, 1912
6. *Empress of Ireland,* St. Lawrence River, 1914
7. *Lusitania,* off Ireland, 1915
8. *Eastland,* Chicago River, 1915
9. *Provence,* Mediteranean, 1916
10. *Hsin Yu,* off China, 1916
11. *Cyclops,* Barbados, 1918
12. *Kawachi,* Japan, 1918
13. *Chaonia,* Strait of Messina, 1919
14. *HongKong,* South China Sea, 1921
15. *Vestris,* off Virginia Capes, 1928
16. *Morro Castle,* off New Jersey, 1934
17. *Squalus,* off New Hampshire, 1939
18. *Thetis,* Irish Sea, 1939
19. *Phenix,* off Indochina, 1939
20. *0-9,* off Maine, 1941
21. *Normandie,* New York City, 1942
22. *Curacao,* off England, 1942

23. Two ammunition ships, California, 1942
24. *Wilhelm Gustloff* and *General Steuben,* off Danzig, 1945
25. *Liberty,* Italy, 1945
26. *Himera,* off Athens, 1947
27. *Joo Maru,* Inland Sea, 1948
28. *Tai Ping,* off Southern China, 1949
29. *Noronic,* Toronto, 1949
30. *Truculent,* Thames Estuary, 1950
31. *Affray,* off Isle of Wight, 1951
32. *Hobson,* Atlantic, 1952
33. South Korean liner, off Pusan, 1953
34. *Monique,* near New Caledonia, 1953
35. *Bennington,* off Rhode Island, 1954
36. *Toya Maru,* Japan, 1954
37. *Andrea Doria,* off Massachusetts, 1956
38. *Eshghabad,* Caspian Sea, 1957
39. *Uskudar,* near Istanbul, 1958
40. *Dara,* Persian Gulf, 1961
41. *Save,* off Mozambique, 1961
42. *Thresher,* off Boston, 1963
43. *Shalom,* off New Jersey, 1964
44. *Yarmouth Castle,* Caribbean, 1965
45. Pakistani launch and steamer, Chandpur Port, 1966
46. Indonesian oil tanker, near Belawan, 1966
47. *Oriskany,* Gulf of Tonkin, 1966
48. *Indian Vessel,* Kosi River, 1966
49. *Heraklion,* Sea of Crete, 1966
50. *Forrestal,* off Vietnam, 1967
51. *Dakar,* Mediterranean, 1968
52. *Minerve,* Mediterranean, 1968
53. *Wahine,* Wellington Harbor, 1968
54. *Scorpion,* off Azores, 1968
55. *Frank E. Evans,* South China Sea, 1968
56. *Namyung Ho,* Korean Straits, 1970
57. *Euridice,* Mediterranean, 1970
58. Two riverboats, Dacca Coast, 1973
59. Overloaded ferryboat, Ecuador Coast, 1973
60. Motor launch, Bangladesh Coast, 1974
61. Two ferries, Hsi River, 1975
62. *George Prince,* Mississippi River, 1976
63. Fleet of cargo boats, Bay of Bengal, 1978
64. Cargo ship and launch, off Bangladesh, 1979

65. Oil drilling rig, China, 1979
66. Oil platform, North Sea, 1980
67. Steamer, Amazon River, 1981
68. Ferry, Java Sea, 1981
69. Overloaded passenger ship, Indonesia, 1981
70. Riverboat, Brazil, 1981